Published in the United Kingdom

GRASPING THE EDGE
© Writers Block, Creative Writing Group
www.writersblockupperbann.co.uk

Editor Philomena Gallagher
Email: philomena1.gallagher@googlemail.com

This book is sold subject to the condition that it shall not, by way of trade or otherwise, be lent, resold, hired out, or otherwise circulated without the publisher's prior consent in any form of binding or cover other than that in which it is published and without a similar condition, including this condition, being imposed on the subsequent purchaser.

First published in paperback in 2009 by Philly Books

Philly Books
18 Bridge Street, Portadown, Co. Armagh, N. Ireland, BT62 1JD
Email: sales@harrisonprint.com

Typeset, Designed and printed by
Harrisons
18 Bridge Street, Portadown, Co. Armagh, N. Ireland, BT62 1JD
Email: sales@harrisonprint.com

Foreword

Hello and welcome to 'Writers Block' Creative writing group' first anthology, 'Grasping the Edge'. This exciting and vibrant new group are the first to be introduced to creative writing through Action Mental Health 'New Horizons' Craigavon and Banbridge as a therapy to aid better mental health and well being.

One has only to read their testimonies to quickly recognise that this art form can have a powerful impact on building confidence; raising self esteem; encouraging positive mental health and well-being.

Their diversity of strengths, styles and interests makes 'Grasping The Edge', a very enlightening and enjoyable read.

How many of us haven't at some time in our life felt we were 'grasping the edge', hanging on by our fingertips just to get through a bad time / stressful time we were experiencing? – yet a percentage of society today still shun those who are experiencing mental health problems.

We all know it is good to talk, yet talking to someone about how you are feeling can be very difficult. 'Writers' Block' members were taught to 'talk to their page'. This takes courage – to spill one's guts on to paper and even more courage to say, 'I am a writer' and go to print! "Creative writing is more than just a means of illuminating memories". "Creative writing engages the heart, the head and the senses to make the whole being sing".

Poetry is about expressing yourself in a way that may inspire someone else. There are no 'essential rules'. It's an art form for self expression – not about counting stanzas or formulating the perfect rhyme.

There was a lot of laughter and a lot of tears weekly – but its therapeutic to have a really good belly laugh and a good cry! Firm supportive friendships were formed and everyone quickly discovered that they all had one thing in common ie their love of language and the care and capability of its use to produce wonderful work. Through various exercises, topics, they gradually unlocked their literacy creativity, shocking themselves at times with the power of their words.

'Creative writing helps me to get things out, get things of my chest. (Christine)

I hope the development of 'Writers' Block' creative writing group can be seen to enhance the growth of creative writing as an excellent form of therapy to aid better understanding of mental health and well being. Their purpose, ie: quality communication in the form of poems, prose and short stories – to celebrate who they are in all their diversities and to encourage all those experiencing mental health problems to come out and speak out, using the medium of creative writing with pride, dignity and beauty, spilling it all; sweet, sour and serious!

Congratulations to all of the group for their thought provoking and inspiring work. This anthology is creative, innovative and imaginative and great credit is due to those who have made it possible. I am honoured and privileged to be their tutor / editor. I am proud of them all. Be proud of yourselves because if your writing is transformed into a book and it touches just one reader by provoking a thought, laughter, tears, any emotion, you can be proud of your accomplishment and consider yourself an author.

Well Done

2009

Authors

Robert Chapman

Christine Abraham

Colin Bleakney

Arlene Finnegan

Tim Higgins

Lynda Ross

Claire Keery

Agnes

Philomena Gallagher

Barbara Steele

Olivia

Acknowledgements

'Writers Block', creative writing group would like to take this opportunity to thank the following:

Southern Health and Social Care Trust

Public Health Agency

Community Development and Health Network for their generous grant, re-Promoting 'Positive Mental and Well Being Small Grants Programme'

Age Concern Help the Aged NI for providing our wonderful tutor / editor Philomena Gallagher, Co-ordinator for Craigavon / Banbridge Ageing Well Health Promotion Project

Action Mental Health New Horizons, Craigavon / Banbridge for all their help and support

Harrison's Print, Portadown for their expertise in printing our anthology

Claire Keery for her art work on our cover and to all those who contributed work

We hope you enjoy our first anthology 'Grasping the Edge'.

ROBERT CHAPMAN
CHAIRPERSON

Testimonies

LYNDA ROSS.

In the ebbs and tides of madness, often the pen scratches its own story.

When I first joined the Action Mental Health Creative Writing Course earlier this year, I was a complete novice. I still consider myself to be so, but I have found that the pen, is mightier than the sword, when it comes to shedding light into the darkness of the mind.

Upon the page battles can be won, problems can be solved, even the impossible can be conquered. But most importantly it is a release, it is a place of comfort, safety and security upon which the best and worst, the real and the surreal can be poured. It is a place where serenity, tolerance, endurance, acceptance and strength can be found.

Writing is an art which I would highly recommend, regardless of age, gender or circumstance. The unsheathing of one's pen in times of turbulence, absurdity, stress, trouble or strife, and the metaphorical 'bleeding' onto page, is one of the greatest gifts I have ever found.

Through the many many miles of ink our little group has grown and blossomed into the "Writers Block." We are honoured to present to you, this our 'fruit' – 'Grasping The Edge.' At times it is bitter-sweet, but at best it is humanity and life upon the page. We bid you taste and enjoy. Do not fear the blade of ink, it is our chosen sword with which to cut through the ups and downs of life.

COLIN BLEAKNEY

The term Creative Writing would have sparked off connotations of writing perfect and rhythmic poetry; since coming to my present class, I am presently and strangely surprised that for me creative writing has enabled me to both voice and vent deep and hidden emotions. Expressing hurt, pain, disappointment and personal tragedy, this for me has been revelatory and therapeutic; no connotations now, just the truth.

OLIVIA.

Joining the creative writing group has been one of the best things I've ever done in my life.
When I was going through many years of abuse and depression I always lifted my pen and wrote poems which enabled me in a safe environment to express my feelings. Though it was only when I met Philomena that I realised how important my poems were to me.
I would highly recommend creative writing to anyone especially those riddled with memories of abuse and depression as it has helped me through a lot.

CHRISTINE ABRAHAM

I have lived with depression for a few years and found it very hard to mix with other people. Action Mental Health offered me a place and I have enjoyed many different courses, taken in a lot of useful information. These courses have helped me take every thing in, were as Creative Writing is totally different it allows me to get things out. Out of my head and unto paper, all my thoughts, feelings and emotions. I have made lots of new friends and we support each other through good and bad times. Creative writing for me has been the high way and by way of my inner self.

Arlene Finnegan

Creative writing gives me a voice and a lifeline. My pen is my own soundboard when the pain can't be told. I have always written my thoughts and feelings down and in my own style I prefer to rhyme.

Within our group setting, a strong recognition of realism is being expressed in different styles and from different observations which is shown within the work. Close friendships have evolved and a better understanding of people and self have become realised.

Agnes

As a child I was a loner.
Affected by a family member committing suicide. I grew up self harming. Married the Bastard. Survived Domestic Violence. Successfully raising three princesses on my own. Accepted my life with a mental illness, rather than living, I have fought every day to fit into Society.
This is the one life you've got; stand for something,
Don't fall for anything. Single parents listen, here it's not who you lie with,
It's who you lie to.

Philomena Gallagher

For me creative writing is the lifeboat on my turbulent sea of life. It carried me safely through adult education, helped me take on board confidence, new friends and a new me, a strong woman who writes her own words, enabling me:
"To sing as if no one is listening; dance as if no one is watching; love as if I have never been hurt."

Robert Chapman

When I was young I had 4 stories published in a book which gave me a taste for writing..... and that great novel that is supposedly in us all has been hiding under the surface ever since. But I never took it any further until I started a creative writing course provided by AMH. During my early days on this course I wrote very humorous poems, but everyone in the group knew I was hiding something behind them....Myself. It is only in the last several months that I have found my poetry allowing my heart to verbalise, and of late I have found myself writing more of life's trials and tragedies. It is an expression of how I have lived and witnessed throughout this life. It is a reflection of me but I have always been guided by light.

When we (the other members of the writing group and myself) are in a room the poems and uniqueness of each person becomes that of a finely tuned orchestra different, important, heartfelt, raw but pure. I am always left wanting more, music to my ears.

These new exceptional family members have made me realise that life has its interruptions, surprises, tragedies and great loves. Each member of our group is completely unique yet the understanding that we have of each other goes far beyond that of any words. We all come from a wide spectrum of this community but fundamentally it is Philomena who is there confidence building nurturing, gradually and lovingly growing us as we get mentally and poetically stronger and this is only the beginning!

Through my poetry I have feared that people will not understand where I have been, where I am now and where I am going but so far they have embraced me and empathised with me more. It's as if I have given it a name and pointed. Now all I want to do is shout look this is who I am take me or leave me but you won't ever be able to ignore the fact that I have arrived........So watch this space

Tim Higgens

As a Christian, I believe everything happens for a reason. I was invited recently to join Writers Block by Philomena at my young stroke club BBQ; I had a severe brain haemorrhage in March, but have recovered miraculously from the seizures and stroke. At first I felt out of sorts with everyone else in Writers Block as I was not from a mental health background, but they all quickly welcomed me into the group, their lunches, and the occasional socialising at their houses. I thought right away that they were having a laughing competition! When I found my old poems to read to the group and include in this anthology with new exercises, I realised that they had been written at a time in my life after I had received counselling for anger management, going back to a traumatic episode in my adult youth. Mental health is something that does affect most, if not all of us, to some degree in our lives! These issues can affect us in so many ways over many years. I am thankful for both my faith in Christ, Who has got me through everything, and the people, family and friends that have been alongside me throughout. I am also glad for the gift of writing, that can express so much that talking cannot, somehow.

As a full-time writer, I have learnt that both inspiration and discipline are needed to accomplish anything forged from words. I have buckets of the former, almost exclusively; I find the collective inspiration within the group and the camaraderie helps redress the balance. I have just achieved my first book, "Able in Christ", a testimony of a good disabled friend of mine. This should now give me the confidence to achieve much more.

I am proud to be included in this group of newly-discovered friends with talents and gifted expression.

CLAIRE KEERY

"I have found creative writing gives me the opportunity to express my innermost thoughts and feelings with those in my group who have an understanding of what I have written. I am hoping that through the publication of this book we can reach out to those, who are in their darkest moments, who will see that there is light, and who will use creative writing to help themselves. My poems have also given me the opportunity to focus on the positives in my life, particularly my children. A reminder that life is good."

BARBARA STEELE

Creative writing for me has been a release, an opportunity to voice the ambitions and experiences that until now remained silent and static. I found initially that my life when penned out on paper had to be disguised, hidden, unacknowledged and unowned, amid emotive sometimes harsh words. Not only have I gained the tools to reach out and be heard and share unattractive depths of myself, I have been able to accept the darker aspects of my being. I know that this darkness can be lightened and relieved when I am able to find the words that alternatively challenge and soothe me.

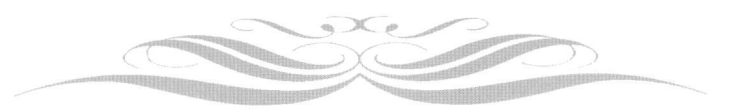

Daddy

It reminded me of you. I remember how you used to tease us with your own renditions of your favourite Irish songs, knowing full well they made us cringe. Don't get me wrong, you definitely had the voice for it, but just the way you looked at us, that teasing grin, your eyes dancing, always finishing with a hearty laugh.

Looking back now I'd give anything to sit by you and have you sing those songs to me. For now I just have to do with the echoes of your voice in my mind.

CLAIRE KEERY

White Steed

Mount a white steed with wings by its side
Fly through the air full of love and pure pride,
Hop on a cloud dance for a while
Slide down a rainbow with a big smile
Feet hit the ground, sweet summer grass
Run like the wind, fast, fast, fast
Jump over a mountain, skim over a sea
Sit on a beach, let the sunshine through me
Swim with the fishes dance with the breeze
As light as a feather, float with ease
Run meet the sunset, welcome it down
Watch with amazement as it hits the ground
Catch me a moonbeam, climb high, high, high
Sit on the moon, watch the world just go by

ARLENE FINNEGAN

Five Months On

Walking by the illuminated windows, excitement ringing in the cold crisp air, she catches sight of her lean figure, the constant reminder of what should have been... five months on.
The baby had been alive, she had witnessed the heartbeat for herself. This precious little life in side of her was alive, struggling to survive.
A week later... no heartbeat, no growth. Her precious little bundle was lifeless. Her baby was gone.
Five months on, festivities all around, the moments of pain are unbearable. The great void in her life lingers. Warm tears caress her cold face. Wiping them away she composes herself. Four other angels need her, for this she must be thankful. She will never forget. Five months on.

CLAIRE KEERY

Horror in the home

He was waiting for me to turn the key
Eerily quiet, next thing a riot
No monster under my bed
This fucking darling wanted me dead
No I love you
Can't wait to see what tomorrow will bring!
No more will I cower to the back of his hand
His lips tight from damming me for breathing
No prince charming tonight!

Horror in my home

AGNES

On My Knees

When life seems so dark,
and all light is gone,
I feel so afraid.
I feel so lost.
When the night closes in,
and all is still,
I feel so tired.
I feel so ill.

Chorus On my knees,
I cry to Thee.
On my knees,
with tears in my eyes.
On my knees,
I plead with Thee,
"Please, help me!"

When my thoughts are confused,
and all sense is gone,
I feel so afraid.
I feel so lost.
When I can take no more,
and I fall down,
I feel so scared,
I feel so alone.

Chorus On my knees,
I cry to Thee.
On my knees,
with tears in my eyes.
On my knees,
I plead with Thee,
"Please, help me!"

When I fall to my knees,
and seek Thy grace,
my heart it bleeds,
My heart it aches.
When all my strength is gone,
and I'm about to give in,
my heart is touched.
I feel warmth within.

Chorus On my knees,
I feel Thy love.
On my knees,
with tears in my eyes.
On my knees,
as I plead with Thee,
I feel thy warm embrace.

CLAIRE KEERY

Childhood Lost

A warning that always comes late
The ominous creak of a door
As light creeps upon the bed
Such a gentle violation of sleep
The child inhales dread through acceptant lips
As small limbs stiffen upon pale pink sheets
The resonating sound of heavy boots
Laces untied.
The grating of a zipper
As panic pulses when the mattress
Dips then settles.
Time to depart for what comes next
The body endures what the mind cannot.
She searches above for angels
Floating on wallpaper clouds
She will play with them till morning
Play away pain-time.
The deceptive silence holds hostage
Echoes of bloodshed and murder
Not the end of a young life, but
The cruelty of a childhood lost.

BARBARA STEELE

A new Spring

Skinny, nimble branches like long narrow fingers
Wave an icy goodbye as I leave forever a winter
Of past regret

I have dared to believe God's Word that
Promises to usher in the eternal miracle of a new
Spring

COLIN BLEAKNEY

A shot from the Dark

Sun surrounds me with feathered fingers
And rests upon my weary brow
Wind caresses my rosy cheeks as it
Whips up around
The cloud above me forms a picture
I see it clear without a sound
Seasons change, colours
alter on the ground
I lie here thinking of the blackness
Time means no more to me as the
leaves ceaselessly meander down
I pull the trigger
hear the sound

CHRISTINE, ARLENE, ROBERT AND LYNDA

Finding the Way

Harmony and happiness light up all the dark
You know heaven isn't just a place for
Those special ones, it may
Come as a shock but if you only
Knock Jesus will hear your sound
And then your life will change
With beauty all around
But the Lord is forgiving and also very kind
The depth of his loving may shock
You first time round, but you
May not know his love is so profound
He shall wrap you in his love
Your feet won't touch the ground
Believe me your life will never be the same

ROBERT CHAPMAN

My Wish

May your days on Earth be many
May your troubles be but few
May God shine His light from Heaven
To guide the way for you
May you never have to wander
Or walk this World alone,
May you always have good health
And a place to call your home.
May your friends stand close beside you
If you ever need a hand
And if by chance you stumble, on a sea of pillows
May you land.
This is my wish for you my friend
I hope it does come true,
I'm a very lucky person to have a friend like you

ARLENE FINNEGAN

Broken Girl

Sleek and straight in full flight
Gliding in, marking out
Open up the splitting skin
On my lord is this a sin?
Silver blade upon my wrist
A hand of God or Devil's fist
Soul abandoned by my fears
My life of woe a stream of tears
Little lines a map does appear
Yells of sorrow no one to hear
Look to see the broken girl
Fidgit heart do not unfurl

AGNES

A Rolling Stone

Dreams and plans once shared
Shattered like minute glass fragments
From a bomb explosion
Memories remain the only baggage
To rebuild a new life
Tears attempt to run, concealing
Hurdles of loneliness from others who
Will never know the depths of this
Chasm. No soul, no roots.
A rolling stone

PHILOMENA GALLAGHER

Lost

Could someone please tell me where is the door?
I've been trapped here so long I can't see anymore.
Could someone please tell me do I need a key
To get out of here, I need to be free.
Could someone please tell me why the pain is so bad
Could someone please tell me am I going mad?
Could someone please come and show me the door
I don't want to be trapped in this place anymore.
Could someone please help me show me what to do
Don't laugh out loud this could be you
Could someone please answer me, is anyone there?
I'm lost in this place, does anyone care?

ARLENE FINNEGAN

Beyond The End (Short Story)

I'm standing at my kitchen bench, no sleep for four days and nights, at last my torment is over. Handpicked pills lay before me; I know which ones will do the job!

For the first time in over two years, I smile a smile of contentment; at last I have figured out what to do to ease my pain. I become elated that I would soon be joined with my sons.

With no thought for anyone else, I make my last cup of tea, light my last cigarette and sit down to enjoy. At that moment I realised I would have to explain my actions to my one and only living child. I went and sought out a pen and paper to write my last letter, the last words I would leave with my daughter. As the pen began to dance on the paper, I had no idea how much this action would change my life forever. Try as I might to explain my actions, I could not find the words that would tell my child that I would rather be dead than be with her. I would die for her but could I live for her? Could I really leave my beautiful, vulnerable precious daughter? Who was I to destroy her world any more than it had been? She had lost too much, could she handle anymore?

The pen jumps from the page, words, sentences flow like a river, still searching never finding the right words. Heart beating, head alert, too alert all hell breaking out, let go, anger raging through me, body jerking, uncontrollable jerking, no peace, no contentment, all gone, just rage and this bastard page. As the minutes, then hours fly by, pen still dancing, hand keeps moving, brain racing out of control. Thousands of words, pages upon pages of my madness, of this hate filled world.

It suddenly dawned on me, as the book flew across the room, by my hand; I was trapped, here in my own snare. I was going nowhere. The moment had passed. I had chosen my path.

As I fell into bed in a heap, exhausted, it dawned on me, did my pen trap me? no! It saved me! My suicide note had become almost a novel! I had found a release - it's in my pen and paper. I guess I chose life.

Arlene Finnegan

A Face

I put a face on to show the world,
The face they want to see.
But deep inside it isn't,
The happy-go-lucky me.
For my heart is breaking deep inside,
The memories I'm finding harder to hide.
As I'm sieving them out a bit at a time,
Trying to say they're no longer mine.
This is easier to say, than to do
As it's me who's had it all to go through.
The pain of rejection, fights and tears,
I've had it all to suffer over the years.
I now want it over and the door closed tight,
For I'm no longer strong enough to face another fight.
I need to be free to star all over again,
And to no longer live my life the same.
Because for so many years what has it done for me?
Just made me sad, lonely and hurt,
For all the world to see.

OLIVIA

A Moth To A Flame

She continues to go back to him,
like a moth to a flame,
and, bystanding, I can see,
she will burn her wings
A little more this time.
Will she ever learn?
Like a moth to a flame.

CLAIRE KEERY

Hannah

Painting in the hallway,
a call from up the stairs,
"Claire, could you please help me?"
a voice with a thousand cares.
Running up as fast as I can
much to my surprise
your head is stuck in the banister
There are tears in your eyes.
I look at you concerned
trying not to laugh
you glance back, so scared
Oh you look so daft!
"What on earth were you doing,
that your head got stuck in there?"
"I don't know, it's not funny,
can you help me Auntie Claire?"
With a shriek of delight
I run for my phone
Camera at the ready
Before the moment has gone
"Oh this is so funny!"
I exclaim while laughing out loud.
You look at me in frustration
Hoping you don't get a crowd.
Of jeering onlookers,
four cousins in a row,
an uncle full of laughter
ready to explode.

I come to your rescue
your head hung in shame
A thirteen year old girl
Hannah is your name.

CLAIRE KEERY

The Note

At the kitchen table I calmly sit
Pen in hand, ready
Glass of water. Previously popped pills
Remembering thoughts of all my ills.
One for every time I cried
One for every time you lied
All the merciless punches and kicks
The constant beatings with sticks.
None for the children I lovingly bore
Grandchildren I totally adore
None for the Lord Who will take me high
He's waiting for me,

GOODBYE.

CHRISTINE ABRAHAM

Protection

I did not really know you
until you were gone
you kept it from us
all those years
loving us
protecting us
if only I had known
I would have understood
I would have protected you.

CLAIRE KEERY

Life's Pattern

Life's pattern formed by mistakes made
Following wrong paths choosing wrong shade
Travelling winding roads not straight
Never happy with what you create.
Always looking for an impossible dream
The perfect special place, beautiful serene
Yearning for that fairytale to come true
It will never happen for me, or you.
Too much time wasted in the wrong direction
Never gained enough knowledge for perfection
Most of life's pattern was lived in a daze
Too late for change, you're now trapped in a maze.

CHRISTINE ABRAHAM

Blatant Words

I remember it as clear as day,
your comment about my size.
I bet , back then, by saying it,
you didn't realise.
That eighteen years down the line,
your words would haunt me still.
Those blatant words, 'you're getting fat',
are they which made me ill.
Today I fight a daily battle,
with food, the enemy.
All because of, way back then,
that comment you made to me.

CLAIRE KEERY

BackDraft

Caught in the backdraft the backdraft of life
As I walk in the door I'm pulled into the strife
The flames they lick o'er me
As I struggle for life
I'm just caught in the backdraft
The backdraft of strife
The flames they burn me
They're burning me deep
The blisters are bursting
But still I don't weep
I pray they move o'er me
So my body can seep
I'm caught in the backdraft
And the burns are so deep
I've curled into a ball now
As flames lick over me
My eyes they are bulging
But still I can see
Sweet Jesus above
It was the backdraft that got me
How could I've missed it?
I just didn't see
Caught in the backdraft
God please come get me
The pain is too great in the
Backdraft you see

ARLENE FINNEGAN

New Life

Sweet soft skin
Glowing
dark blue eyes
Searching
Tiny tender heart
beating

CLAIRE KEERY

All I want

As I sit watching the world go by
I am lost in myself.
Physically trembling.
Waiting for the food to kick in.
Energy gone.
What have I done to my body?
Guilt engulfs me.
No escape.
Failure in trying.
Will I ever be able to eat
without counting every calorie?
Wanting to restrict,
throwing up?
Who am I?
Is true happiness being content in your own skin?
Loving yourself no matter what your size and shape?
This is all I want….
To be truly happy.

CLAIRE KEERY

Wheel of Life

The potters wheel spinning
Slow, steady, shaping, demanding
His wishes. Faster it spins, smoothing
Out cracks and blemishes
To his desires. Soft pliable clay
Collapses

PHILOMENA GALLAGHER

Andy

Brave young soldier
barely an adult
eyesight lost
missing limbs.
No magic wand
no return.

What determination
through months of pain!
Emotional rollercoaster.
Mother's distress,
birth of a beautiful son.

These are not tears of pity.
They're of deep gratitude
for young men
like you
who show such courage,
such amazing strength!
Resilience.

The meaning of hero?

You!

Thank you.

CLAIRE KEERY

My Prayer

As I stand before my maker
I pray mercy he will show
And take pity on this mortal
Who does not know where she'll go.

There's times I've been so harsh
And times I've been pure bad
Times I've been so happy
And times I've been so sad
Times of trials and heartache
Times of Evilness

The rage it pumped right through me
I wore it like a crest
The smile I painted on
I laughed it off with jest
But the monster lay there in me
I was on a quest

The devil came right in me
I tried to cast him out,
My god was right there with me
Of this I have no doubt

He took my hand and led me
To a safer place
I can say in honesty
That I have seen god's grace

I hope in all my torment
God will see some good
And give me another chance
To prove if ask I would

I pray for his forgiveness
I pray he'll take me in
I pray he will not cast me out
Into a sea of smouldering sin

ARLENE FINNEGAN

Rainbows

Wellington boots,
waterproofs,
dancing in the rain.
Climbing trees,
in the breeze,
like Tarzan and Jane.
Mountain bikes,
baby trikes,
playing out for hours.
Nature walks,
tiny talks,
picking mummy's flowers.
Gathering sticks,
magic tricks,
rainbows up above.
Stories read,
prayers said,
a camping trip full of love.

CLAIRE KEERY

Mounting of Testing

The ice can spike and the wind can shrill
But a walk in their face can still be a thrill,
If only I push on through at my will
And reach the bliss where their temper is still.

Or at least to the summit while their fevers still rage,
And elation of conquest is tenacity's wage:
Though the gale may still howl, victory will assuage
And the descent transcribe to a different page.

TIM HIGGINS

Calling in the night

It's dark and eerie the place I go
When things get uptight
It's far away, a secret place
Deep inside the cavern of my mind
So quiet, a stone echoes through
Skipping across a pool
Too much for me to take
Run away I must, find a safe
Haven until dark
Wrap up in a blanket, sleep away the fuss
Happiness of someone cares, calling in
The night, answer to help them in their plight
Will I be able to fight through a crappy
Cluttered mind?
Cry for help louder, they must be near
A soul in pain, sounding sincere
What if they don't get through
Stay safe behind the blanket of my
Mind
Calling in the night

ROBERT CHAPMAN

Writers' Block

Poetry read
Words said
Emotions felt
Hearts melt
Ears listen
Eyes glisten
Eternal bonds made.

CLAIRE KEERY

The Dreaming

Cold clawing evil
Trapped in living hell
with livid eyes
you bare down on me.
I submit to your awful will
And let you sin upon me.
I leave my mind
And sail in oceans shores,
dance upon the desert hills
walk among the dead.

LYNDA ROSS

Another Day

I don't need you to fight my corner; I'll fight it on my own
I know you want to help me, but my friend we fight alone.
For in this world of trouble, misery and pain,
We must learn to fight our corner, again, again, again
If I let you fight my corner, then the oppositions won
And I never will again hand them a loaded gun
Please do not be offended at what I have to say
But you have to understand I must fight another day.
The power that I have now I fought so hard to get
The pain I endured I never will forget
The price of power was costly; it brought me to my knees
It took my World and crushed it like some obscure disease
I guess what I am saying this battle is my own
And no-one else can fight my corner I must fight it all alone.

ARLENE FINNEGAN

Horror at the Home

He mentally tortured her for years
She left she couldn't take any more
Now he mentally tortures his three year daughter
Uses her as a weapon he's truly rotten to the core.
He sees his kids two days a week
Bribes them with toys and sweets
He never wanted his children before
He just likes to see their Mother weep.
Without sleep, totally stressed, she can't believe
He's dragging her through court today
To achieve what she doesn't know
Horror at the home forever
He plans to make her pay.

CHRISTINE ABRAHAM

Last Night's Storm

Beautiful, young tree
bent and broken,
arms tumbling to the ground.
Yesterday,
full of life,
tall and proud,
elegantly sweeping the sky.
Today,
lifeless.
Beaten by last night's storm.

CLAIRE KEERY

Pretty In Pink

I stand here in my new dress mum and dad bought the other day
It really is quite pretty, even if I do say
It's pink with white polka dots, just like my sisters face covered in spots
She is seventeen you know, almost a woman now
Wouldn't wear a pink and white dress, no, denims she likes best
The tightest jeans in the land go right up to her armpits
At least that's what mum said the other day
It's strange how I feel now, it's as if I've gone away
I'm not that happy little girl, they had before
I shy away from everyone, my Aunts and Uncles want to know why I sit alone.
I can't tell them all what's wrong I have to deal
with it on my own. Big sis well, she doesn't want to know.
She just wants to hear her music, that heavy metal on the radio
Why would she care? It's over for her, she's not worrying anymore
It's me who has the woe to get through each day
Why does my MUMMY touch me there whenever dads away?
It hurts so much I could scream and scream, but sure

WHO WOULD BELIEVE ME ANYWAY?

ROBERT CHAPMAN

Alone

You turned your back on me today
For once I stood my ground
Huffing and putting won't knock me down
No peace will you conjure up
Hold back your love
How is it working for you?
Head in hands won't ease my hell
Standing alone, betrayed, forlorn

AGNES

The Moses Basket

Why did you do that?
Why did she ask?!
Heart aching,
Stomach churning.
Wanting to scream,
"it was for my baby, not hers!!"
Nausea
Head spinning
Hands trembling
I wasn't ready to let go….

CLAIRE KEERY

Invitation

If by chance you pass me stop and say hello
Don't be in such a hurry to get where you may go
For I am here forever lying in the ground
The people here beside me never make a sound

I was once like you my friend scurrying around
Till one day I didn't see the truck that laid me in the ground
So take the time to savour, have a chat with me
Rest your weary bones awhile, take in what you might see

For life is just a moment, a moment here in time
Enjoy your moment well my friend
It's sad but I missed mine

ARLENE FINNEGAN

Why

Older than her years
Thin wrinkled pale.
Chair in the corner, she crouches,
Hi ya, with her voice so frail.

No electrics to be touched
Meals on wheels for her
Microwaveable in minutes
Needs no shaking or stir

Devastated family look on
She lives her life at ease
How the hell did my sister
Get Alzheimer's disease?

CHRISTINE ABRAHAM

Porcelain Cold

You carried me in your womb
Unwanted,
Pushed me into this world and
Away,
Waited in vain for love to arrive
Denied,
Access to constant silence,
Deprived,
Tears flowed, hot, salty,
Unstrained.
Sat alone watched you
Porcelain cold

PHILOMENA GALLAGHER

The Diagnosis

The young man sat on the edge of the treatment room bed, legs swinging listlessly to and fro' the fear of what was to happen eating away at his mind, slowly and methodically eating its way through his brain. Forty minutes had now passed since the good looking nurse in her white tunic and navy trousers passed through the ominous looking grey door, sending his life into a spiraling deep depression the likes, of which he had never faced before, at least not in this world. How, How would he brake this devastating, earth shattering, ball breaking news to his wife? Was there any way he could do this gently? No how could you ever do this gently? Just tell the truth, that's the way to go with this. Now wait a minute though, is that the way to go? Nah this needs dressing up. Such a situation needed tact and decorum. Now how to go about it that was the problem! I could play the sad card, but it was the hardest one to play, you really had to mean it to get away with it, be dramatic but be careful not to over dramatise, that would definitely give you away, too many "so sorry" and "I didn't want to hurt you" wouldn't cut the cake. I never seemed to learn from my mistakes and there had been too many of them to mess up now. No this needed quick, careful and forthright planning. To get away with such a crime would be a master stroke if I could pull it off. Maybe you could help me reader, I would be forever in you debt? Oh what's that you say "what is my dilemma?" Sorry have I not mentioned it thus far, well I suppose I thought it was obvious, but here goes.......

I will be curious, nah gripped to hear your answer so

HOW DO YOU TELL SOMEONE YOU HAVE JUST EATEN THE LAST ROLO?

ROBERT CHAPMAN

Death by Mother

As he walked across broken glass
His feet crunched out the sound of one
Too many arguments
People thought better not to interfere
As he beat her to the ground
Light and harmony has gone
Once illustrious surrounds, now only the
Smell of the dead seeps up through this
Dark and rotting ground
Shock! How the ambiance has changed the
Smile upon his face as if nothing at all
Has changed but the beauty has gone from
That lifeless soul that lies upon the floor.
No more children will she mother or fondle to
Her breast
No growing pains
No party games
Just a lifeless crushed out face
Lies in a dark and dreary room
No more children will ever leave her tender
womb - and what about the
Baby left lonely in the crib -
When its mother
popped those filthy pills?

ROBERT CHAPMAN

In Sympathy

Your loss
will be
but a moment
of the eternities
you will share.

CLAIRE KEERY

Wanderer

I looked straight up, into the sky
And saw a satellite passing by
Whisking across the specks on soot
A beacon of life without any root.

Spinning silently, with no care
Yet sending its signals to who knows where
Or maybe the tin can has finished its task
And ploughs through the void as a funeral cask?

The speed it must move and the sights that it sees
I wonder if I could escape through the trees
To its solitary path 'round this glowing ball
Reflecting the sunlight, seen by all
Who would chance to look or care to espy
This occasional visitor to their piece of sky.

To fly through the nil and look down below
And marvel at creation's splendrous halo;
Mountains, deserts, forests in shrouds
Of wispy, fleeting and mingling clouds.

For perhaps a day, spinning blue and green
'Til I'd had enough of all that could be seen
For loneliness is unkind; while creative and pure
It can lead to thoughts, moods and feelings insecure.

My words may seem glib, my ponderings twee
But one of the truths experience shows me
Is that no man's an island, and though he may choose
To be a lone wanderer, he never must lose
Sight of the fact that if the satellite would pause,
It would blend with the pattern of the starry gauze.

Tim Higgins

The Walls

If walls could talk they'd say,
get a life, you sit all day
and right through the night.
Why not show us you from outside?
Let us see you in day's sunlight.
We know you so well, both inside and out
we have our tricks and we'll play them out.
We will close around you and bring ceiling down,
meet you with floor and trap you throughout.
You only think you own us you know
it is us in control and we never move.
You can alter our colour and give pattern or two,
but you cannot change our masterly post.
We are the ones that play in your head,
we have ears but lucky for you,
we are without tongue.

LYNDA ROSS

Rhythm

My heart it is beating
The rhythm is wrong
It hasn't been the same since you are gone
You left in a hurry you just went from this place
God how I miss the sight of your face.
The way that you held your beautiful head
I remember you sleeping as a baby in bed.
The first time I saw you my heart filed with joy
Our hearts were in rhythm my beautiful boy.
Right through your lifetime you always stayed close
I never asked why? I just made the most
The day that you left me my heart missed a beat
The rhythm is wrong

It's now incomplete

ARLENE FINNEGAN

The Rose

How pretty sits the rose
gentle, unimposing, harmless.
Beauty grace in petals rest.
Yet behind the pretty fascade
lies a depth of darkest sin
for on its stem lies thorns
that draw the blood within.
How beauty often is
the darkest evil in.
How softly on the eye rests
but wicked in the heart,
the rose its beauty wild,
but with its price you die
for all its gentle side
below the beast doth lie.

Lynda Ross

Better Late Than Never

I was anxious and seething with anger. How could he be so casual about tonight? Late again, getting through to that man was like grasping water.
I'm curious to hear the excuse this time, I feel like calling him to tell him not to bother coming home. I slapped on the TV so hard I nearly broke it I thought this was so funny I laughed.
There was a pile up on the M1, a man in a black Chrysler 300 appeared to be speeding and crashed into an overtaking lorry. The man was pronounced dead at the scene.
The door bell rang and the smile ran from my face.

Christine Abraham

No Fairy Godmother

Dorothy isn't in Kansas
She's out somewhere in Iraq
Her red shoes are army boots
All splattered with blood.
The yellow brick road is still there, but it's dusty.
Desert and mine filled land,
all littered with vehicles burnt out and blown up.
There is no fairy Godmother.
She forgot to turn up for the party, she's elsewhere
drinking gin and smoking.
Her eyes have rolled behind her lids and a little drool
has escaped from 'tween her lips.
For Dorothy there's really
no place like home but she'll not see hers again.
For an M16 awaits her soon.
One shot in the hip and one in the throat, poor Dorothy.
She won't float, she'll lay like disused carpet
on a bed of golden sand,
her blood spilt like rose petals
browning in the sun.
Poor Dorothy, better you'd stayed in Kansas.
Why fight a war in a far away land.
No thanks you got,
just lead and heat.
Your demise a waste in the dusty landscape.
But you'll be remembered
for a little while least.
Poor little Dorothy
and no red shoes
to save your 'sole'

LYNDA ROSS

Alone

Cold
Alone
By herself
No happiness
Life's love fell apart
One cup, one saucer, plate
Freedom's door now opened wide
The world was always her oyster
A breath of fresh air swept through her life
To work or retire, to pause or to play

Not answerable to anyone again
Woman does not live by bread alone
One bad apple does not ruin life
Forgive and forget, he begs
No rock to lean upon
No comforting hand
Isolation
By herself
Alone
HURT

Philomena Gallagher

Matthew

When I look at you
I am reminded of all the beautiful things in life,
Flowers, butterflies, sunshine, rainbows.
In an ever darkening world
it's easy to lose sight of these things,
but as long as I have you,
I have light,
I have hope,
I have everything.

Claire Keery

Insecurities

Does my bum look big in this?
Does this hide my obscenely big belly?
Is this dress too low for the show?
Should I wear these shoes or those?
Does my hair look alright, I just had it done?
Would anyone notice if I wore slippers to drive?
Is that girl in the shop prettier than I?
Would you fuck J-Lo if she gave you the eye?
Can he see the stretch marks all over my thigh?
Don't look at me, I feel fat today,
I can't wear that it's the wrong time of the month.
Look at my hair, it just won't behave.
Why do the other mums look better than me?
How can I look good? I haven't got time.
Hey, why do you never say you love me?
Is this skirt too short for my stumpy legs?
Do these boots make my calves look massive?
You're always so passive, would it hurt you
to say, hey darling, you're looking good today?
Would anyone notice if I slipped out a fart?
What do you want, that I dress like a tart?
When will that guy finally notice me?
Why, right after, do you roll over and sleep?
Are my arms too fat for that sleeveless dress?
Is my cellulite worse than it was last week?
Does my bum look big in this?

Yes dear, it does
and yes, it is.

LYNDA ROSS

I Don't want to Remember Him

I don't want to remember him.
How we sat in his kitchen,
His son, my friend and I, with him
over coffee
and laughed until midnight.
I don't want to; not now.

I don't want to remember him.
The night my car broke down,
he came out and towed me back
to his garage. In the pit
we worked until 2am.
On that freezing night
until that clutch was fixed.
I don't want to; not now.

I don't want to remember him.
How he laughed and laughed
at my Halloween costume;
A home-made 'Cousin It',
and joined in the fun.
The coolest dad I knew then.
I don't want to; not now.

I don't want to remember him.
How his daughter, in our band,
practising in his attic,
wanted to sing "Oh, Daddy" to him.
I don't want to; not now.
Not now I know what things he did,
in the dark,
to his own children.

TIM HIGGINS

Chip On My Shoulder

A chip on my shoulder, I carry about
Only one on view but this one I flout
Well time is no healer, no healer at all
On my day of beginning, I stumbled did fall
When abused by the few, they were close ones you see
No one could have believed, sure it is only me
From trouble and strife to repercussions and pain
My life has been in a circle, again and again
When I was an adult, anger, confusion I held within
Self loathing and despair no one could dim
Seared with medications of all kinds, the answers all here
When you walk in my shoes, then you will see clear
My madness is not badness, as I'm justified
You see I met some bad people and they told me lies
So I carry it with me, the madness I mean
The slate well I've tried there is no wiping it clean

AGNES

Refuge

My safety arrives with darkness.
Shadows provide my salvation,
They embrace my weeping body,
Cleansing open festering wounds.
They are not able to heal my mind.

My refuge is born from anguish.
I go inside where no-one can reach me.
I can observe the room below,
The people cannot see me,
Yet I witness what they say and do.

My refuge is chased by the cruel dawn.
I must return to face another day,
I spend it yearning for my consoling,
Comforting darkness

BARBARA STEELE.

Don't forget to breathe

It's with a heavy heart I write this,
I don't know what to say,
My heart is breaking for you,
In every kind of way,
The place where you are standing,
Is a place where I once stood,
The people gathered with you mean no harm,
Just good,
The things they are saying,
Will make your body seethe
The only thing I can say,
Is don't forget to breathe,
I'll call with you tomorrow I cannot call today,
I can't watch your loved one being carried away.
I ask for your forgiveness I don't want to make you seethe,
Remember what I said my friend,

Don't forget to breathe
(Dedicated to Lisa)

Arlene Finnegan

The Wardrobe

Radio blurring, television on.
Every one talking a load of shit.
Drinking coffee dishes strewn.
Left for me to tidy it.
Children pulling out cupboards and drawers.
Demanding biscuits, sweets and drink.
Taking off their shoes and socks.
"Mum could you check if he's done a stink"?
Head dizzy, spinning round and round.
Like countries on a globe.
I need to leave before I go mad.
You'll find me in the solace of my wardrobe.

Christine Abraham

Walk Tall

Walk tall, my friend, that's what
They say
I walk taller than you any day
What's that you say?
I'm only four foot eight not even
The height of a snooker cue!
What you don't see; I walk with
The Lord, eight foot tall and more
He fills my heart, he swells my mind
He is in my life all the time
What's that you say.... does it not bother
Me to have on board some company
Does he not fill my mind and mess with me
Does he not drive me to insanity?
He walks beside me everywhere, gives me
Help when in despair. He holds me together
When no one else is there, he always
Answers my every prayer
Jesus said, "Walk tall my friend"
Walk tall beside me
Never hang your head in shame; I'll
Be there to take the call, just
Keep on walking tall,
I'll cleanse your deeds, crimes and all
There is no need for your head to fall
I died for you upon the cross
So you will never, never be lost
Walk with God

Walk Tall

Robert Chapman

My Baby

It's 2a.m.
I wake to you,
calling in the night.
"Daddy! Mummy!"
"Mummy! Daddy!"
I crawl out of bed,
half lost in sleep.
I open your door.
You are there,
welcoming me.
My baby.
I love you.

CLAIRE KEERY

Greatest Moments

Pain of a woman
Lonely road ahead
Dancing with life
Applauding the dead.
Forgetting the past
Beauty of life
Hurts of friendship
Trouble and strife.
No butterflies dancing
Lost first love
My greatest moment
Moving above

CHRISTINE ABRAHAM

Letting Go

Stephen I promised you some words a line or two
This is serious, The Lord has spoken
To me, yes this is no bluff, now why he
Did this I'll never know but the answer to your
Question a lot of fathers need to know

He said and I quote

"I know you love your two daughters
You watch them blossom and grow
They're two fine young girls for in them
My love you have sown, you're a
Wonderful father and this they both know
But a time in your life will come when you will come
To me and say "Father I love them, When do I let go?
Children they are no longer
So please let me know when oh when do I let go"?
Well Stephen the answers simple just let their
Lives flow for inside them my love still doth grow
"But Father when do I let go?
Stephen for this question the answer you already know

FOR IN THIS YOUR GOD'S LIFETIME
THERE IS NO LETTING GO

Robert Chapman

Dedicated to Stephen Keery

Hands

As I look at my hands what do I see, they look very old and wrinkled to me.
These hands once belonged to a child, carefree and happy just moving wild skipping and drawing as
life passed her by never asking the question, Why oh God Why?

Then they passed to a young lady you see it's strange to remember that young lady was me
These hands were hard working they never were done,
They dance and they played, they had so much fun,

They passed on to mother and wife as they held my babies I start a new life.
Gentle and kind filled with love hope and joy,
What a beautiful time I just sat back to enjoy.
They held three of my babies now one of them gone.
God bless him and keep him my baby John.

Again these hands had a new role, still gentle and kind but, something was stole.
These hands became protecting and pushing away, her husband was first, he didn't go easy that's all I can say

After thirteen years together and two children to boot.
he got the message and just slung his hook,
One girl of twelve and a boy just ten, these hands picked up the pieces and started again,
These hands didn't miss him over the years they had held back his anger and dried up the tears

Same hands went on daily without even a care, whenever I needed them these hands they were there,
These hands took a phone call one summer night, they drove to the Hospital shaking with fright,
Hands covered my eyes so I couldn't see what was so plain in front of me.
Hands covered my ears so I couldn't hear; hands went to my eyes to dry up my tears.
Hands clung to my daughter as we said a prayer, these hands have never failed me they've
always been there.

ARLENE FINNEGAN

Dear Mum

As a child I stood silent and still
Hoping that you would see through that veil of fear,
Hear my silent cry for help that danced
On the tip of my tongue
As you prepared for his great coming
A solitary immaculately be suited
Uncle Jack
Would throw me over his knee
Slap my bum
Make me sit astride
Rock back and forth
Rub his jagged beardy face
Over mine,
Force his foul tongue into my ear,
And my mouth, and he, he …..
While humming his silly song.
You would laugh and say
Uncle Jack loves you
Be a good girl, play with Uncle Jack

PHILOMENA GALLAGHER

Depths of Despair

Depths of pain and despair
Go far beyond
Death is dark, depression lurks
Everything closing in
Deaths dark grip, a deathly grin
Ashes to ashes, dust to dust
No razor blades or hang mans rope
There is always hope
Life may be grim
To hell and back
See it through, reach for my hand
Live to fight another day and
The devil be damned.

ROBERT CHAPMAN

Phone Call

Sobbing, Sorry, sorry,
Are you Christopher's mum?
Yes, why?
He's been stabbed
No, no, he's downstairs
Please get to Daisy Hill
Hospital now.
Within nine minutes
His Dad meets me
Time means nothing
Doctor tries to speak
I yell, get back in there
Do your fucking job
Don't talk, go, go, save
My son.
I'm sorry, he says
All hell breaks loose
Beginning of the snowball

Police, detectives, talking, talking
You have to identify the body
My son, my handsome seventeen
Year old son
He's yellow, tubes everywhere
Everywhere tubes
Ordered don't touch, evidence
I need to hold him
What undertaker? Remains
Must go to Forstergreen
Remains? That's my son!
Family arrives, tears
Snowball starts to roll.

People, people, keep coming
The funeral, more people
People everywhere, press scramble
Police, people, stretching three
Miles, shops, pubs, closed
Graveyard full with people

I'm lost in the crowd
I want to scream
My son, mine, leave, go home
Snowball gathering speed.

House full of people
Not a word spoke
I go upstairs, lie down
People, all I hear is people
Open my eyes, it's dark
Silence.
Gather the will to go downstairs
More people
Put on the mask
Snowball rolling faster

Control stolen
Decisions made for me
People. Police, victims, this
Victims that, no time
No where to hide, no peace
No sleep, no food
No Christopher!
Where is my life?
No answers, no time, no Peace
Totally helpless
In limbo
Explain again, again and
Again
Where's Christopher?
I don't understand
Chrisy – Chrisy!
No answers, no answers
People staring
When will Chrisy be home?
No answers, just people
People, people
   Snowball out of control

ARLENE FINNEGAN

Love's Path – The Prayer

Bent, broken, bloodied, twisted,
I claw my way to hallowed ground.
Are you the quay that will make me free?
I turn to you in prayer and hope,
lift the darkness and lay me in light.
Let me heal in warmth and love
not drown in this my deepest plight.
Lay hands on me that I may cope
with all that life delivers on me.
Let me walk within your past,
hold me close within the cold.
Show me sights in forgotten path
but give me future within a grasp.
For all I hope and all I dream
let it be done beside thee.
In gentle jest, hold me blessed-
Without you, I am so much less.

Lynda Ross

Loneliness

Dreams once shared
Shattered like shrapnel
In an explosion.
Memories remain the only
Baggage to rebuild a life
No one will know the depths
Of this chasm

Philomena Gallagher

I Want

Independence, respect
Love that never ends
Family appreciation
True loving friends
Do what I want
Freedom to come and go
Nobody to answer to
Mix with people I don't know
Space of my own
Shinny and clean
Peace and quiet
Happier than I've ever been.

CHRISTINE ABRAHAM

Ride the Storm

Heart pounding, head aching
Mind running scared as ugly
Sharp hurtful words rained
Heavily, chipping away at all
Defence, drenching in guilt and
Shame. Anger flashing cold blue
And sharp red as she attempted
To run for cover with only
Prayers and silent pleas to defend
Herself. She had made her rich
Gold autumn bed and now had
To lie on a cold dull dove
Grey tear stained mattress and
Ride the storm

PHILOMENA GALLAGHER

Herself

Lanterns lit the dining room
Everything in place
All she had to do
Fit in that damm dress!
Material, stubborn, would not budge
Don't rip the cream lace
Pulling here, pulling there
Sucking in; holding breath;
Turning like a bloody rubic cube
No matter how she struggled
Just couldn't make it fit
She would have to puke some more
Like she had done everyday before.
Now a size six
Nothing any doctor could fix
Whom would she displease?

Herself

ROBERT CHAPMAN

Deepest Depth

.... An unexpected cunning fog
Wrapped itself tightly around
Enveloped and held fast, draining away
Feelings, joys, plans. Suffocated thoughts
Actions. Sucked away all colour and light
Delivered insecurities, mocked all senses
Vulnerable to past histories I obediently
Followed and wallowed in its deepest
Depth

PHILOMENA GALLAGHER

Butterflies Dancing

Butterflies dancing on a sweet summer breeze.
Like two a penny down do they fall.
Down to the flowers all pretty and neat
for the nectar to sup without defeat.
How they flutter and shimmer in summer heat,
without thought nor care, oh what a feat,
to watch butterflies dancing on a sweet summer breeze.
It makes me go weak, right to my knees,
all colour and gaity, supple yet strong
the butterflies dance all day long.
But I have a question about them all.
Where do they go when night doth fall?

LYNDA ROSS

Grasping The Edge

I'm holding on so tightly, My knuckles white with pain
If my grip should slacken then I will go insane
My heart is just a tether, A little piece of string
Holding tightly to my mind, the key to everything
But if the string should slacken, Or even break in two
I'd tumble into wilderness, What am I to do?

So as I'm grasping tightly to the edge of everything
I won't ask much of you my friend perhaps a prayer you'll bring
Please pray that I will not let go and never lose my grasp until my
life is over when I can rest at last

ARLENE FINNEGAN

Mirror Image

Studies her reflection
Counts ribs one, two, three
Hip bones jut out for all to see
Collar bones easily traced
Breast bone, lonely.
Stick thin arms hang limply by
Her side
Young heart hurting inside.
Fragile thigh bones stifle flesh
Ankle bones, just sharp rocks.
In her mirror image, she's beautiful
Fits into place, belongs to the human race
Smiles shyly
Whispers weakly
'All the King's men couldn't put
Humpty together again'

PHILOMENA GALLAGHER

Untold Story

A great big gap in this world of mine
You'd think I'd learn with passing time
The world it runs riot in my mind
It's been doing that for a long, long time
Each day a story doth unfold
A story never to be told
Dark and dour; please god don't let
It unfold – my life would explode!
I want to kill you: It is your time
Your life must end before
Abusing me, again, again, and again

ROBERT CHAPMAN

HE

My parents don't understand me sometimes
But then neither did His sometimes.

I've faced hostility
He did too.

I've had to suffer weddings
Like He did, at least once.

I've spoken to crowds
He knew all about that.

I wondered if they really heard
I wonder if He pondered that.

But crowds aren't what I want
He seemed to tire of them too.

Peace and quiet is vital to my life
He also had that need.

He was rejected
As I have been.

He was misunderstood.
I always have that problem.

He was betrayed.
I do know something of that.

But He had a few close friends.
I thank the Lord for mine.

They did leave Him though, when He needed them.
I too have felt alone, though maybe without reason.

I love to walk in gardens and forests.
He spent precious moments in a garden.

I love to sail across a lake
As He had to do at times.

I really like climbing mountains and hills.
He climbed a hill, once too often.

TIM HIGGINS

Love

It brings out the beauty in people
the smiles
the gentle stares
the compassion
if only we could all experience some love in our lives,
maybe we wouldn't be compelled to do
some of the things we do.

CLAIRE KEERY

The Web

Memories put away like old
Tilly lamps. Dust gathering slowly
To cover all scars, dry up all juices
Waiting patiently, expectantly, for the
Years to stir the ashes
A delicate lacy web of deceit
Tangled you but set me free

PHILOMENA GALLAGHER

Roy

Here we are today,
you over there,
and I over here.
Memories fading fast.
Desperately holding on.
Missing you.
Life passes by.
Each second one less,
of time spent together.
I'm glad we have forever.

CLAIRE KEERY

Life's Pattern

No poetry
No liers
Don't tell me your tired
No rubbish
No throne
No memories of home

Now it's all in the past
I want to get a chance to ask
The man at the top
Why it didn't stop
Wrapped in a wooden box
Plastic luggage for the trip
No tea for me to sip
It's gone, gone, gone, gone

No shepherd
No blame
Don't hold unto shame
No kicks
No laughs
No bubble baths

Now it's all in the past
I want to get a chance to ask
The man at the top
Why it didn't stop
Wrapped in a wooden box
Plastic luggage for the trip
No tea for me to sip
It's gone, gone, gone, gone

No end
No bend
No tucked in shirt
No scribe
No love
There wasn't a dove

Now it's all in the past
I want to get a chance to ask
The man at the top
Why it didn't stop
Wrapped in a wooden box
Plastic luggage for the trip
No tea for me to sip
It's gone, gone, gone, gone

AGNES

I Wonder

I'll always wonder
What life would've been?
Having a mother
So alive, so keen
Someone to call Mummy
Comfort me, Cuddle, kiss
Sit me on her knee
Friend to talk to
When I'm feeling down
I'd have been so proud
To walk with you in town
Someone to help with
My wedding day
Enjoy my children
Criticise, have your say
I know there's a reason
Why God took us apart
You'll always have a place
In my memory,
In my heart

CHRISTINE ABRAHAM

Crescents of Pain

Enfolded securely, warmly embraced
Absorbing the essence of strength
Corded muscles flex and protect
Helping to hold back the gasps
Tears and curls mingle freely
Navigating a separate path
Boldly you expose tortured skin
Imprinted crescents of pain
My fingertips will gladly blend
The vivid crimson stains of blood.
A gentle, tender kiss will heal,
Heal the skin, but not heart.

BARBARA STEELE.

Eileen

A gym slip mum.
That's what they called me,
all satchel and bump,
knocked up at thirteen.
I bore the disapproval,
was worse than your birth,
the tut tuts, the glances,
even strangers did glare.
Look at me all satchel and bump.
But I'd prove them wrong,
I'd be the very best mum.
Give you love and good care
like any other new mum.
Be proud pusher of pram,
all smiles for late feeds.
Look at me now, all satchel and bump.
Judge not thou my fate
nor stare agate.
My rape it was short,
but I have since it forgot
when I looked down upon,
my bonny Eileen.

LYNDA ROSS

A day I'll always remember

More black clouds appearing on high.
Rain pours viciously from dark sky.
Complete silence except for shuffling feet.
Great respect, weeping discreet.
How could they! Put him in that hole.
Deep, wet narrow and cold.
I'll never forget feeling so sad.
That cold wet day I buried my Dad.

CHRISTINE ABRAHAM

Letter about the Lavey Lovey?

Where's the letter about the levy on the lavey lovey?
Oh the letter about the levy on the lavey lovey is in the lavey lovey
What's the letter all about anyway lovey?
It's all about the council placing a levy on the local lavey lovey
But why do they want to levy the local lavey lovey?
Possibly to levy more money out of the local lavey, lovey
But wheres the envelope that held the letter about the levy on the local lavey lovey?
I think the envelope that held the letter about the levy on the local lavey is in the livey lovey
How did the letter about the levy on the local lavey become separated from the envelope that
held the letter about the levy on the local lavey and ended up in the livey lovey?
I don't know lovey, all I know is that I'm reading the letter about the levy on the local lavey
lovey and I'm not in the livey lovey, I'm in the lavey, Lovey!

COLIN BLEAKNEY

April 15, 1912

You shudder on impact
Hit on the side and going down by the bow
Lifeboats fan out, like injured swans afloat
While the violins sing,' Nearer thy God to thee
Descending from the world
Cradling over a thousand souls
The merciless icy waters
Deliver you

BARBARA STEELE

Grasping The Edge

Dark coven, I hang upon the precipice
Grasping the edge with tortured fingers,
Let not I fall among their midst
Where to shreds my body rips.
Utter not no sound from lips
Let me hold fast to my grip.
Raise me up upon thy wing
From this the haven of noir.
I hear below the horror choir,
Chant and verse of deepest curse.
It is the place of murdered souls,
Of tortured spirits and underlings.
I grasp the edge with fervency,
Feel my flesh it liveth still.
To all as sundry I do call
Let not my horror be this fall.
Let me live and I'll forgive.
Rend not me from my mortal shell,
I will show you I can give.
I will cast upon the dark
A light so bright it'll shatter all.
Upon this second chance
I to Earth do deftly haul,
For into hell I did not fall
And now I give my very all.

Lynda Ross.

Bubbles

Light,
airy,
drifting in harmony,
the beauty,
the ambience,
Bubbles.

Claire Keery

Dirty old Town

Beauteous girl, she smiles at me
My heart pounding for all to see
Such beauty doesn't often come round
My dark and lonely little town
Like lantern lit she flits round
A ballet dancer, makes no sound
The perfect picture I have found
She has put life back in the dirty
Old town
How can I win her to be solely mine
And keep her close for all time?

CHRISTINE, ARLENE, ROBERT AND LYNDA

My Whispers

As I lie in my bed I hear whispers,
Whispers that come in the night
Whispers of comfort and sorrow,
Whispers that say it's all right,
Whispers that tell me it's over
The nightmares have passed for a while
Whispers to say please stop crying it's alright
If you want to smile; these whispers
They come in the night time they only
Come after dark, these whispers they're sent
Here to help me, a new life perhaps I'll embark
But for now I'll hold onto the whispers
The small voices that speak in my ear
Whenever the whole world is sleeping
My whispers, they speak out so clear.

ARLENE FINNEGAN.

Ruined Poetry

Binding love forged with golden rings
Scattered jealousy seeds firmly rooted,
Shreds of kindness, trust honesty,
fell like petals of wreaths blown
across the earth. Copious tears
Isolation, Accusations, Stirred
the Ashes of Ruined Poetry
New woman writes her own words.

PHILOMENA GALLAGHER

Stolen

Who could tell where life would take me
Inside this wild and crazy mind
As roses drop their petaled blood
My lacerated body who will find
As life slowly slips from me for
No one cares for this lonely child
Orphaned by this world unkind
Only God will ease my mind

CHRISTINE, ARLENE, ROBERT AND LYNDA

Tears

Trying to hold back
Eventually I give in
Appearing like A fool
Releasing my pent-up emotions
Somehow bringing healing

COLIN BLEAKNEY

Unfailing

These mountains are so vast,
So anchored yet so free.
Lying under sunrise, sunset,
And all that's in between.
The challenge of the scaling
Of the incline of the ground
Is my soul's solo calling,
Always skyward, homeward bound.

Clear morning air,
Cool dawning light,
Mellows the heather's woody coarse.
The warming stair
Of the sun's flight
Lightens and lathers rigour and gorse.

Climbing up their incline,
The brush of herb on boot.
The sphagnum squelch is strangely
Warm and soothing underfoot.
Rush of river's water,
Endless flux of roar,
Overlaying silence
Which the birdsong will restore.

Tight gasping breast,
Taut sinewed force
Power the drive to drive to the top.
Soon dawning crest
Of struggle's divorce
Romances my strive to unfail and not stop.

TIM HIGGINS
(MOURNE MOUNTAINS)

Bring Them Home!!
(In memory of Sean).

Weekend news:
TWO MORE BRITISH SOLDIERS
KILLED IN AFGHANISTAN.

Headlines the same from week to week.
Young adults giving their lives.
For what?!
'Greater love hath no man than this.'
"Bring them home!!" A widow's plea.
Are you listening Gordon Brown?
If he was yours what would you do?
Our sons and daughters,
our brothers and sisters,
Our mothers.
Our fathers.
How many more will we lose,
before you make that call?
Bring them home,
to our soil,
where they belong.

CLAIRE KEERY

The Whirlwind Ends

Thoughts a whirlwind in my head
From early morning till bed
Can't string thoughts together
Words tickling my mind like feathers.

Thoughts obstructing my brain
Letters floating like the finest grain
Forming words that make no sense
Black fog appearing cold dense.

Close my eyes try relaxing
Thoughts pounding my mind distracting
Stop this whirlwind.
Everything will be dispersing with this head.

CHRISTINE ABRAHAM

Life

No one knows the pain I hold,
Yet I know to get better the truth must unfold.
This is easy to say, yet so hard to do,
As I have to discuss what I went through.
You've ruined my life more than you'll ever know,
I just wish I'd had the strength to tell you to go.
But I didn't, I was terrified of you,
So hell on earth I had to go through.
I had nowhere to run, or anyone to say,
What was happening day after day.
The guilt and shame I live with each day,
No matter how hard I try, it doesn't go away.
Yes I can push it over to one side,
Until a flashback appears, then there's nowhere to hide.
Now it' time for make or break,
Not only for myself, but my husband's sake.
You've taken my past, future and life,
Each day stopping me being a proper wife.
I can't let you rob any more from me
It's time I accept help to set me free.

OLIVIA

Pain

How you burn my very soul
With those bony icy fingers,
Ripping through every sinew
Tearing apart my very nerves.
Trapped inside this square circle,
Spinning round without escape.
I burn, I bleed, I bruise, I scream
Soundless in the night.

LYNDA ROSS.

The veiled Box

The veiled box cannot be opened
Too bright, the light inside does blind
Screaming thunder vehemence engulf
Its fetor snides impetuous

The veiled box has sought imposters
There lateral advances scorned away
Melancholy constricted their swallow
Prepared the necropolis for me

The veiled box has no analgesic
Misery, torment hysteria and injury
Grab all the memories incaptured there
Leave me and my casket abandoned

AGNES

Shalom

Happiness without contentment
is a yacht becalmed in blissful weather
when you'd rather be at the shore.

Contentment without happiness
is sailing safely through the storm
knowing the shore is in sight.

Neither is realising you're lost at sea.

But both is seeing the coastline,
then peacefully steering the boat
the other way.

TIM HIGGINS

Wrists

Watch the moon going down
My face doth frown
Dusk Envelopes Mountains
This blood stains
Sweat slowly seeps
Skin on my body creeps
Try not to inhale
Again, in this I fail
Come sleep perfect sleep
No tears will I weep
Sliding away, peacefully low
Pain I won't have to tow
Blood lies in black pools
Nobodies fool
Reach into the earth
My life of still birth
This surety is comfort
Life I wanted to abort
Demons cover the damage done
Won't trouble friends by using the phone

AGNES

The Whisper

My heart, it plays one last fit
Deep below in this dark crypt
My body not yet stripped
Lonely I here sit
My mind demands one last trip
Before my blood gives final drip
Your name I whisper on my lip

CHRISTINE, ARLENE, ROBERT AND LYNDA

Soul

Tell me what is a soul?
If everyone has one, were is mine?
Does it have a gender, is it female like me?
How is she attached to me, is there an invisible thread?
Is she that distorted shadow who stalks my every step so silently?
Is she that imaginary friend who struggled through childhood with me?
Does she disapprove of every lie I have ever told?
Does she know the answers that are so yearned for yet remain elusive?
Does she hold memory within her greedy, selfish grasp?
Does she dwell between the realm of spirit and faith?
Is she the bridge that spans life and death?
Is she that moment when my lungs capture their last breath?
Or is she that rattle that resides within the throat of final darkness.

BARBARA STEELE

The Child Within

I reach for you but cannot find,
I buried you so deep inside
never letting you laugh and shout,
making you hide for fear and doubt.
And now, at last, I let you out.
See around you, all about.
Play with glee cos you are free
and at last you can be,
a proper part of you and me.

LYNDA ROSS

Willow

Young, growing tall
Witnessing the turn of blackened reborn skies
Cowering branches relent and bow.
Muddy earth is dappled with lost russet and gold
Cast down by a swift, mercenary autumn breeze.
Soon snowflakes hug each vulnerable, naked limb.
Creating a pure protective womb
Seasons define growth, grief and rebirth
Winter bequeaths release.
Sunshine filters through the frosty haze
Allowing the cathartic flow of tears
The weeping willow
Weeps

BARBARA STEELE

Whispers of Love / Hate

Your whispers were in my ear and with a look or
Stare
I know how to behave, what it was you needed, little
Did for me you care

Your whispers fell of your tongue laddened with your
Hate
Lies and danger stung my mind, faces crimice with your
Bile be back, DON'T BE LATE

Your whispers were predictable a safe place for me
To be
I knew to jump and run and fetch, to heel,
With a movement of one finger your love! Please
Stop I'd plea

AGNES

Hands

His hands were hard and very strong
I knew on me they didn't belong.
Two hands pinned me firmly to the wall
I hadn't the strength to even call.
But if I had've who would have heard?
There was no one around,
He had the last word.
So totally weak, frozen in fear
The regrets I now live with year after year.
If only his hands I could've pushed away
Maybe things would be different for me today.
This is something I'll never know
So on with life I have to go.
But before I do, if someone is hurting today
Please seek help, don't let them have their way.
For the nightmares will haunt you right to the end
And it's a long road to recovery for your heart to mend.

OLIVIA

Spoiled

Spare the rod
Spoil the child
Lashings of tongue
Repeated kicks
Black and blue
"Honour your Father"
you would say
my soul crept out
of me and away

PHILOMENA GALLAGHER

Comfort is

Comfort is:
The perfection of a mesmerizing star filled sky.
The angry fierce fire that dispels a persistent chill
The larger hand which swallows mine and helps me
Chase away despair.
The innocence in a child's laughter
The heavy secure bolt across my door
The weight and warmth of a purring cat
The escapism achieved when engrossed in a good book.
The kinship felt when someone can understand the demons
That devour and torment.
The knowledge that when I close my eyes at night, darkness
Is only temporary
The assurance of a God that loves and forgives
The friendship that grows and endures

Comfort is:
The bonds of friendship that we bind with love

BARBARA STEELE.

Through the Mind of a Child

Covered in measles
Poor little tot,
She peers through the bars
Of her little wooden cot.

"Where's my Mummy?"
Haven't seen her today,
Mummy's not coming
Angels took her away!

CHRISTINE ABRAHAM

Broken

My heart is broken and totally sore,
Please, dear God, I can take no more.
Stop this abuse, give me a light I can see,
So I finally can be set free.
From all the memories that run me down,
Making me wish I was six foot underground.
Yes, I get up every day, saying
I'll put it to one side.
Then a flashback comes,
I rush and hide.
I need to realise I have so much to live for,
A lovely husband and nieces I adore.
They're the only things in life,
Keeping me alive today.
So I thank God immensely,
For sending them my way.

OLIVIA

To Please

You're stupid and thick, just like your dad.
These comments daily made me sad.
Can you do no right at all?
Comments like this made me feel small.
So constantly I tried to do my best,
But each time the goals were moved,
So I failed the test.
So every day through the year,
I always tried deep in fear,
To do my best knowing I'd fail from the start,
Yet another knife would go through the heart.
No matter how hard I tried every day,
I never gave up trying to please her someday.
But now it's time to call it a day,
Beginning to do things all my way.

OLIVIA

Flawed

I know of the comfort in darkness
Of sleep continually denied
I know of the eye and pallor
A canvas stretched taut and stark
An aftermath, perhaps
Evidence left behind.

When the role I play is redundant
The faces dissolved already, dispersed.
I endure the aching moments, until
My leaden lashes sweep and dip
Spiked by liquid acid, it often seems.

I wait as my comfort dances and dims
Eaten once again by ravenous, neon dawns
Baptised hand in hand with fragrant
Magnolia soap, bathed and fortified
I emerge, hallowed almost bodiless
Confronting this flawed, brave new day

BARBARA STEELE

Calling In The Night

Lying here all alone, solitary heartbeats.
I miss your touch and limbs all tangled
In loves inter-locked web,
No-one knows where each body ends.
Your name I find myself calling in the night,
Where are you so far from sight.
It cannot be true, just doesn't seem right.
By my side you should be,
From morning til night, together entwined
till dawns soft light.

LYNDA ROSS.

Is feeling believing?

To feel is to experience
To experience is to believe
To believe is to trust
To trust is to hope
To hope is to wish
To wish is to want
To want is to need
To need is to possess
To possess is to have
To have is to own
To own is to feel

AGNES

Pact Undone

Pen its hot, molten words
Tempers singe to the core.
No time now, just let rip
Think through later, repent.
Words like shards deep thrown
Cuts to bone and tear stain.
Sorrow after, too late done.
Damage wrecked loves arbour.
No more standing hand to hand,
Grasp ripped in broken land.
No think first before the act,
The pact undone and shadow cast.
Sweet love do forgive
The moment's heat, the fuel spilt.
Grace be good, let it weep
And blessing keep. Forgive me love.

BY LYNDA ROSS.

Tomorrow

It no longer hangs in the sky.
She opens the door,
inviting the darkness into the room,
welcoming the cold silence.
She walks over to the dresser,
stoops low,
and lifts out the small red book
from its hiding place.

Pen touches paper,
words flow,
writing away the anxieties
brought on by the first glimpse of the sun.
Laying them to rest,
for a short time,
all is well.

Sleep.

Tomorrow,
is another day.

CLAIRE KEERY

My greatest moment

Learning to dance in your arms
Firm hold on my heart
Beating music, feet move in turn
Around the floor unto the path of life
Knowing with surety the steps to take
Not being laid, stepping together
Toward my greatest moment

AGNES

Sand

In the sand I wrote, a face I drew
To tell the world what my heart knew
One of the things I count as true.

Knowing that within the day
The tide would turn and wash away
The candid disclosure I could not say.

Was this the whole, the full-blown truth?
Discovered, emerging from my youth.
Now thirty, my novice wisdom uncouth.

For the sand does shift, it comes and goes
With no volition in the ebbs and flows
And no ambition to interpose
Any objection to the merciless tide
Its arranged, surrendered, unwilling bride
In whom only a fool would dare confide.

Since the sea shall sequester every script
And drag it out to its ranging crypt
'Til all intent from its spirit is stripped.

Then devoid and vacant, without worth,
Thrown back to where it had its birth
But strewn across a wider girth.

Taking my stick, I wrote more words
Only to be seen by passing birds
And solely by the breeze to be heard.

Hoping that this other fact
Would be taken by the sea intact
Added to the first in pact
And someday to my world brought back.

Belief, unless by rock is breached
Will meld with other grains of beach.
Then other truths will come along
And together write another song.

TIM HIGGINS

Woodland

I crush the long green blades beneath.
My heart makes- love to another.
Leaves scamper playfully,
distantly
The shadowed weight above,
obliterates a dying sky
I am consumed by salvation
and of passion, reborn.

Trees so tall, with their beseeching
barren branches,......stretching.
Perhaps they feel my need for comfort.
I am sheltered, protected by a blanket of bark,
lying underneath on a mattress of feathered leaves.
The branches sway in an almost silent song,
swooning with sorrow in softest lament.

The passion fades too swiftly,
before my shadow rises
I gaze once again at my escaping sky,
Soon my tiny beacons will appear,
bringing a radiance of luminous light
I hear the sounds of ruffled clothing,
the zipper grates and offends my senses.
My shadow is considerate, he leaves me,
so I can welcome another soothing twilight.

BARBARA STEELE.

Chinese New Year

Rubics cube coloured dancing dragons
Brightly lit lanterns of red and gold
Traditional Chinese dress, satin costumes
Celebrations for young and old.

Indulge in Chinese cuisine banquet
Displace bad thoughts enjoy
Forces of Chinese spirits
GONG SEE FAA CHOI.

CHRISTINE ABRAHAM

No More

I speak no more
Time passes like broken glass,
Red welts turn to blue.
I drop my eyes, no more reprise.
My sin you accuse
Home ten minutes late.
Any excuse for lash and bash.
An animal I wed
And took to my bed.
I loved you once,
Now I despise
Fear and retreat.
Live life in silence
Afraid to speak,
Not antagonise
No threat am I,
Quiet and small
Beaten to the wall.
Time and time again it passes
Like broken glass, I wait next time.

LYNDA ROSS.

In a Ball

Curled in a ball, I'd cry at night,
Having been hurt in another fight.
I was helpless and couldn't fight back,
I knew if I did she would break my neck.
So I stood as a punch bag and took it all,
With nowhere to turn and no one to call.
I just kept praying it would end,
So my heart would gradually begin to mend.
But my prayers weren't answered, it just went on,
I just asked God, where have you gone?
Why, God, do I suffer so much pain?
What does it achieve? What does it gain?
I could keep asking questions, but where would they end?
For the answers I'll never get, to help my heart mend.

OLIVIA

The Mask

Misery how it compounds,
The awful bloody truth.
I cannot breathe
Can only weep.
I am a broken doll
Limbs in tatters,
Mind it shattered.
Inward focus, sword and bow
Slashing, piercing, cutting me
Round and round this bloody dream,
There is no end it would seem.
Try a smile to hide behind.
It'll do for me.

BY LYNDA ROSS.

Grim

Ashen fingers grasping me
Tearing flesh, rotten core.
The bad apple fallen
Stinking awful bloody gore.
Drowning in this comatose
Life has stopped, pulses dead.
I want grateful death instead.
Standing still, clock is broke
Time so still, none awoke.
Grey suits grind the day away,
Til the ground their situ meet.
I watch you all, but do not feel.
I am the soul reaper & include you.

LYNDA ROSS.

Grasping the Edge

I'm grasping the edge
I don't want to let go
My ship is sinking
To the dark depths below
Don't want to go back there
Bad feelings, desperate thought
Not knowing whether I'm coming or going
Where I've been or what I've bought
Grasping on and fighting back
Kicking and screaming I'll get to my knees
I know I can get help and support now
I will stand again, take my hand please.

CHRISTINE ABRAHAM.

Diamond Necklace

She entered the room, the diamond suspended by the fine gold chain was unmistakable. There was no question that this was a real diamond for as it caught the light a brilliant multivaceted coloured flash pierced every eye, twinkling, sparkling and flashing, almost as beautiful as the one wearing it.

Heads turned as the door opened, it seemed that every eye was transfixed upon her beautiful face, her cheery smile and her elegant stance. She wore a deep purple dress and velvet purple shoes, she was indeed a picture of beauty. But is was her face, her cheeky, cheery smile and her wavy jet-black hair that distinguished her as her eyes glanced around the room, roaming, looking and searching.

Finally she caught his eye, he had spotted her first, his gaze intently and excitedly fixed on her smile, then at her face and then finally on her eyes.

She was the one alright ...

Her smile became so much more rich, meaningful and beautiful as they both looked at one another. She observed specifically that he had noticed her beautiful diamond necklace and he likewise observed that she had noticed the brilliant yellow daffodil protruding from his top pocket.

At that moment they exchanged smiles, smiles that conveyed and exchanged a thousand memories. How could she ever forget?

She had been a waitress at a café in a remote seaside village and he had been a travelling inspector for a prestigious group of Hotels. He loved his job for it took him all over the world travelling to top resorts, dining in the best restaurants and enjoying the good life. But off late he couldn't help but feeling that something was missing.

He was feeling more and more unhappy and less and less fulfilled, life had become predictable, routine and consequently boring. This had caused him to become somewhat cynical the message

on his t-shirt said it all,
"Seen it, Done it & Now I'm wearing the T-Shirt".

It was the T-Shirt he was wearing as he entered the café that beautiful spring morning. He had been lured into the shop by the smell of fresh pastry and the aroma of freshly roasted coffee. As he waited to be served, he read a newspaper.

"Seen and done what?" came a question in broken English.
"I said, Seen and done what?" the question came again

I'm sorry, I didn't notice you, he replied, I was so engrossed in this paper. Well, eh, the T-Shirt ... oh yeah that one he stammered. She looked at him and giggled, her hand momentarily covering her mouth, then resting on the table where he was sat. It was then that he noticed her smile, wow, she was beautiful.

At that moment he impulsively did something he never thought he would have done in his life, he asked her to sit down beside him and join him for coffee. "Oh I cannot, I'm sorry, if I do I will loose my job", she said.

"Well then, what time do you finish?" he asked. "Half past five," she replied, as she smiled again, you can meet me here". "Yeah, yeah, fine", he said, eh doesn't matter about coffee, but I will be here for five thirty, see you then". Avorre, she said, smiling again.

He left the shop feeling and hearing his heart beat, no actually I'ts thumping he told himself. His breath was short and shallow and his legs were like jelly. He took a deep breath of sea-air and steadied himself.

His immediate thought was to get back to the Hotel as quickly as possible, he knew he had his best pair of trousers his trendy jacket with him.

"I'll have to dress to impress", he thought.

At last five thirty arrived, he was there standing at the door, watching, waiting and looking for any sign of her. The door opened and out she came her hair flowing in the gentle breeze, and with that unmistakable smile.

"Hi," he said nervously, how are you? She giggled again, her hand going up momentarily to her mouth, "I'm fine," she replied, how are you?" "Oh yeah, great, great, he replied, I suppose your hungry, would you like to go somewhere to eat?" "Yes, OK" she said, "I know somewhere good, just overlooking the sea at the top of the town". "Sounds good," he said, "let's go".

An hour later Kevin was sharing his story with Carla, telling her about himself, his business trip and generally about his lifestyle. He turned his head again to admire their commanding view of the sea, then turning his eyes back to Carla again he observed her beautiful smile again.

He took one of her hands and with his other hand touched her long fingers, then looking again at her face he impulsively got up out of his chair pulled Carla's chair back and lifted her to her feet. He held her waist gently and pulled her toward his body, then looking at her beautiful lips, he kissed her.

This was no ordinary kiss, this was beautiful, intimate, heavenly. "I've something to tell you", Kevin said, I will be leaving tomorrow at lunch time to travel home to the UK, but will you promise me something?" "Yes of course," she said

"Will you come with me tomorrow morning for a spin out into the country?" "Yes, I'd love to", she said, in fact I know a lovely place not far from here by a river, we could have breakfast there, would you like that?" "Great, we'll meet tomorrow then", said Kevin

Early the next morning, Kevin handed Carla a black velvet box, inside was the most beautiful necklace Carla had ever seen, a beautiful diamond sparkled and flashed with a blinding brilliance as she suspected it in the air. She sat breathless, "but, why, why did you…" Before she could finish her sentence, Kevin put three fingers gently over her lips.

"Sush," he said, "listen, now here's my proposition Carla, would you promise me you will wear this necklace for me at our engagement party?" Carla stared at him in disbelief, "but, but we've only just …"

"I know, I know", said Kevin, "I know all of that, but just hear me out, I have arranged to be back again next month, a room has been booked in the Hotel where I am staying, I would like you to arrange to bring whoever you want to attend and I'll bring some guests, and if your wearing the necklace, I'll take it you know it's right for us to be engaged, but if not, we will just continue to date if that's ok by you?"

Carla impulsively turned around and plucked a bright yellow daffodil and said to Kevin, "Well then, if you believe it's right for us then will you wear this daffodil to the party?"

"Yes, yes I will," said Kevin

The month of March passed by very slowly for both of them.

They kept in contact via email and by phone.

At last the day came, Kevin had flown over with a party of guests, there they sat in a room making small chat but filled with anticipation.

As Kevin watched the handle of the door turn and Carla entering, this was the moment he had been waiting for, immediately he got up from his chair and made his way to his beautiful Carla.

She was wearing the necklace with the brilliant flashing diamond.

Kevin looked lovingly and kindly into Carla's eyes, and as they embraced, a daffodil fell from his pocket.

COLIN BLEAKNEY

WASP

Little wasp, annoying wasp,
Buzzing 'round my head.
A magazine! I roll it up
And swing it. SPLAT! You're dead.

TIM HIGGINS

The Unwanted Guest

Lying in bed curled up in a ball,
Quietly waiting to hear the call.
Are you up, it's time you were?
But it didn't matter, he was there.
In he crawled under the cover,
And to him I was nothing but his lover.
The child in me fell into place,
As he came in close to my face.
Inside my head was saying, go away,
While praying, please God, not more today.
He did things that hurt me deep inside,
But I had to be strong, I couldn't have cried.
He pawed, poked, squeezed so tight,
While I lay helpless and couldn't fight.
My voice was gone, I just wish I could've said,
Please, please, just get out of my bed.
But, as so often, I just lay in shame and pain,
Knowing tomorrow it would happen again.

OLIVIA

Forgetting the past

Always a gun at my head
This body would freeze in that bed
Smell off his odour, listening to his venom
I plead he won't inhale
We need to run
Run run out into the freedom.
Unknown is a warmer, safer place
I can't forget the past
Bleak and black, berretta and bastard
No more cold temples for me.

AGNES

The Family Photo

The photo hangs upon the wall, for everyone to see,
Mum, dad, three children, the perfect family.
But if they could only see what was happening day by day,
They then would look at the photo, in a completely different way.
As daily, I would rock side by side, trying my tears so hard to hide.
Laughing and joking for all to see,
How well the world was treating me.
This was how people had to see my life,
They had no idea of the family strife.
The beatings, rows I face every day,
Knowing the silence always must stay,
Behind closed doors firmly shut tight.
No one must know things aren't right.
For it wouldn't look good, if the church would see,
How really hard they were treating me.
When bruises appeared a story was made,
While I prayed hard for them to fade.
Dad just kept warning, no one must know,
Or into care I would go.
The emotional scars are still raw today,
Leaving me wondering, will they ever go away?
It's a true saying, no one knows what goes on behind a closed door,
But thank God for me I don't have to suffer anymore!

OLIVIA

Friend

If I were to ask just one question of you
Could you honestly answer no need to refer?
No open heart surgery, the answer is there
If I was to open my heart to you
Could you hold gently on, not waver on queue?
Would you stoke away sadness?
Could you see me through?
Would you stand beside me honest and true?

AGNES

Why, God?

Curled up in bed crying to my bear,
I prayed to God, are you there?
If you are please come to me,
And please, please God, set me free.
From all the pain I suffer most days,
Coming at me in different ways.
Through words, thumps and a squealing voice,
How then, dear Lord, do I rejoice?
In a wonderful world, I just can't see,
But why Lord? Is it just me?
What have I done wrong, to hurt me so much?
Can you not just grant me a gentle touch?
Or even a kind word, that would mean the world to me,
And finally, to know I am now set free.

OLIVIA

I will never forget

Emotionally lifeless and physically bruised
I started to take back for all that I loose
Taking back my power leaving out your greed
Holding onto others that's the void in my need
You've not enough understanding, patience or time
I've no one to shoulder this enemy, is mine
To go back is to hold on, so I'll fly and I'll go
Your not fit to shoulder this burden, only a human,
Not a friend
You've lead me down the path where the sign said
Descend
Well I'm not so clever, no riches or gold
Just let me tell you I've no wish to reload
So I'll be happy alone, not sick with you
I'm changing the pattern, in fact,
FUCK YOU

AGNES

Pain

The sun, for a change, is shining today,
So I have a lot to live for, you all might say.
But today I'm crippled with a lot of pain,
It's taking all my strength just to stay sane.
I feel so old and totally done,
My life's lost it's hope and all the fun.
'Cause pain runs me down,
Day after day.
I ask God, what else is coming my way?
It isn't for me to question why,
So I carry on with one big sigh.
Swallowing tablets one after one,
How long will this go on for,
Until my race is run?
God I should be grateful,
For what you've given me,
But just at the minute,
It's hard to see.
All the qualities in life,
I have to live for,
As they seem so far away, because I'm so sore.
So at the end, weak from another day,
I pray, God please help me to see,
How much in life,
There is really meant for me.

OLIVIA

Belladonna

Soldering on knees, nothing can please
Irritant become terminal, epicentre chastened
Soul subdued, epilogue engraved on my charnel
House, finalized the epistemology of hurt
Warm me belladonna

AGNES

Mobile Phones

What would happen if all the satellites fell out of the sky?
Would the art of communication die?
Would people stop saying goodbye?
Do you think peopke would find it harder to lie?
Would anyone be able to look anyone else in the eye?
Would people know what to do and where to go?
Do you think friends would bother to show?
Would worlds collide, people still meet and know how to greet?
Could we all cope without delete and send as our best friend?
Would people talk to each other as they walked instead of talking to their mobile friend?
Would the world as we know it come to an end?
Would the atmosphere become our friend?
Would everyone forget text/send?
How would everyone get on if the art of communication was to end?
Tell me my friend could we survive without our mobile friend?

ROBERT CHAPMAN

Loss

Feelings of loss, dreams all gone,
Deep in my heart I'll always long.
For the children I never will bear,
To hold so tightly and always care.
For all their needs in daily life,
Protecting them from any strife.
Giving them love fully each day,
Knowing they're wanted in every way.
For me this is a dream I never will know,
As others watch their children grow.

OLIVIA

May

May is coming, my stomach's in knots,
As soon there'll be five full cots.
Five smiling families spilling with joy,
As proudly they announce, it's a girl or a boy.
Cradling their babies proud they should be,
But it breaks my heart to watch and see.
As the days follow it'll be all baby talk,
When they first smile and begin to walk.
These are memories they'll treasure forever,
As I sit back knowing for us it'll be never.
Jealous I'm not, just broken and sore,
For I'd have loved the chance for a baby to adore.

OLIVIA

Lonely road

Keeping this heart beating, no-one left seating
Hoping for a crumb, not with any old bum
Have you anything to be had, my heart is sad
Could we go out for a curry?
With your imminent health worry

AGNES

The Wind and the Waves

If the waves were listened to as they crash in rhythm
Are to be thought of as pages turning
And if the wind turning those pages whisper also
The words of my days
Then let the wind and the waves be silent for my
Life is spent

COLIN BLEAKNEY

The Day I Will Never Forget (09 April 1997)

I went to bed well on time the night before
So that 5am would not catch me too early
Up I got, the house so quiet and eerie
The rooms all empty of life

Soon that would be filled with a beautiful wife
and plenty of life, I ate my breakfast
and brushed my teeth I hate that feeling
of grit on my teeth

Grabbed my helmet, my bike suit on
Out the door to the bike, Oh how it shone
Climbed on the mean machine the engine roared
Out the gate the throttle I floored
This motorbike I loved I really adored

Off to work on my beautiful bike I tore
Arriving at work I felt so good
for working I was really in the mood

So in the doors to the changing room
boiler suit and hairnet on
clocking in the work begun

Down to the chill room it's always so cold
I started the boxes to check and so
 started this day I would never forget

The day rolled on the craic was great
We needed pallets for those deliveries to load
So I volunteered, the sun split the skies
We all enjoyed some time outside

So on the forklift I would ride

My life a turn for the worse
it was about to take
the shit was about to hit the fan
My friend life as I knew it was about to end

Isn't it funny how life doesn't always pan out
As we planned? Life doesn't give a damn
He doesn't care when his hand he bends
What way your life may end
The back of the lorry was getting close
Soon to real work I'd have to go

The next thought going through me is why did he do that?
I shout this out as I scream and scream
No passing out for poor old me
I was in FUCKING pain you know what I mean

The forklift driver he didn't move
I lay on the pallet all battered and bruised
I thought of my wedding, what would I do?
Laying on that pallet all battered and blue

The secretary arrived with her lame idea
Let's move him she said, but a friend
Who was sane, on the pallet let me
stay until the ambulance came

I knew a leg was broke for sure
Something the doctor would have to cure
I lay there in agony upon the bed
In my mind my life was at an end

A broken leg a great big hole
Now the dreaded diabetes
would take its deadly toll

And what was I thinking about
but my intended beau

I thought how I had ruined her big day

The pain was really grating in
the effect of pain relief wearing thin
Do you know what it's like?
Four breaks: a hole: I thought
someone had ripped out my soul

Now in the ambulance
Why was time talking so long to pass?
Even though we travelled so fast
To the City Hospital we did fly
A hundred miles an hour now that was some ride
I didn't even know when we had arrived

Up to the ward I did go
So many questions they had to go slow
Lucky my beau was there to help
she did everything a future wife could

Eventually the nurses came to take
Me down to the chopping board or theatre to
those who don't know the rooms

Two doctors were sent
to fix me they were intent
two brothers, their father
Arch Bishop of Armagh.

With mallets and drills
They began to put me right
The nails were driven right through me
Then began to screw
Sounds like they had been to B&Q

Believe me, two and a half foot nails through your bones
Would make even the strongest man moan
Of the hole, they had to leave it alone.

I woke next day up on the ward
But of that day I shall tell no more
Except to take a bow because
I have two legs, at least

I DO FOR NOW

Robert Chapman

The Whisper

Salt upon my wounds you pour
With sweetest lisping drooling words.
I see your lips, so soft, so warm,
Like they could melt the artic walls.
In softest whisper lent my ear
Your breath a rose upon my throat,
Gentle petals tickle me
But thorns they pluck in deep.
For words not in lullaby shed,
But darkest threat upon me lash.
You with all your modesty,
Play out the graceful pantomime,
But hide behind the beauty glamour.
You are the beast that roves awild
Your game I see with all too clear,
The tinted specs I leave behind.
You are the gilded lily,
With scent that suffocates,
Robs of sense and life you dash.
You are the whisper, the succubus.

Lynda Ross.

The Sea and Me

The sea that goes around the world
Has come back again today.
To all the other shores she's shingled
I wish she'd carry me away.

She slithers daily down the beach
Yet returns to it in waves.
So feminine, she can't decide:
I can't grasp how she behaves.

If I had the chance to run away
I presume I might just go.
But stronger ties of loyalty
Form the only way I know.

The dichotomy of what I want
In life is always there;
To divulge and do just what I want
Or to yield and humbly serve.

To yield is often portrayed
As a soft and feminine trait,
But the greatest man did yield his life
To a painful, shameful fate.

My thoughts will always be plagued
By the doubts and fears of life.
My walk will follow all the roads
Of both victory and strife.

I am just like the ocean
In all her ebbs and flows
And the even keel that I like
Is lost in my toss and throws.

I suppose I'm not the man
I'd really like to believe
But in me is a man
In whom I can believe.

TIM HIGGINS

Grasping the Edge

Hanging by fingertips
Blood mingling with ageing stone
Wall of life painfully crumbling
Tsunami of vile hateful, abusing
Accussing words attempts again
And again to drag body and
Soul to oblivion
Tempting to 'let go let God'

PHILOMENA GALLAGHER

Butterflies in Flight

When I'm surrounded by people but feel so alone
When my path is unclear and so far from home
When the noise won't stop and the winds on my face
Look to my Lord his presents bring grace

When life's fabric is woven then frays at the seams
When a plan falls apart and ends the dreams
When the water is murky the choice is unclear
Look to my Lord he'll draw us near

When my friend is a foe eyes sting with a tear
When my burdens are buried with a new one I fear
When it's all too much and I need to go
Look to my Lord he lifts up high from low

Chorus
Hosanna, Hosanna, butterflies in flight
Hosanna, Hosanna, stars, twinkle at night
Hosanna, Hosanna, his love givith me
Hosanna, Hosanna, his name is our victory

AGNES

Murder of souls

A slap not a tickle
Scream not a giggle
Punch instead of a lunch
Shattered glass under foot crunch crunch
Run for you a bath with bubbles
Longing for gentle cuddles
Insult and injuries
Nothing I do can please
When did it all go wrong
Long before you came along
Sigh let out then I did quiver
Your voice, your smell makes me shiver
Cold and alone, lonely afraid
Wishing me gone wishing me dead
If it wasn't for you well where would
I be
You showing me right from wrong ohh yes
I do see
Bring me hell in dark of night
No one to tell of this my blight
Isolation, betrayal its nothing new
You've brought me to heel on the end of
Your shoe
Clean, wipe, brush, dust to keep it
Nice
My tardiness came with a price
Your dinner, your lunch, coffee and tea
Walk past the mirrors I don't dare
See me
Keep quiet, shut up, get going
You've gone
Play happy families all at once
Then you'll fawn
No card, no prayer, no love not for me
Please don't have this game as your
Last plea

AGNES

Three Clerihews

Jeremy Paxman
is known to be deadpan,
But this can bely
how his humour is dry.

Stephen Hawking
has difficulty talking.
But never mind,
His brain is just fine.

Gordon Brown
has a terrible frown.
But his attempt at a smile
is worse by a mile!

TIM HIGGINS

Wardrobe

Between the doors there stands a mirror
Look beyond the glass, what can you see?
Two sides to this person but all you see is glee
Stare closely, now feel my pain, it's the last call for plea

Beside the mirror stands two doors with handles
Hanging there
To open wide reveals too much just don't stand
And glare
Feel the cotton shirt, the christening gown that each
Baby once did wear
Next to it there is a blouse that in his
Jealousy did tear

On the top shelf is the jumpers I did fold
Little notes for mothers day warm me in the cold
I'm broke and empty, a nuisance, well in this I know
I'm told
I want to stay inside this wardrobe
That gun to my head, some day will explode

AGNES

LIFE TRILOGY:

A day i'll never forget

How blessed I am!
We are.
How blessed we are indeed!
So many lost so much
So many times.
Yet that day,
despite my wife's berserk call,
the manic moment,
the furious drive from work to the hospital,
the beseeching petitions to heaven,
she was fine.
Our daughter had not drowned.

A day i'll never remember

The seizures came so suddenly.
Standing in church
Then the paramedic.
Then the ambulance;
its vaguely darkened windows.
Nothing more.
"They had to sedate you,"
a friend told me later.
Think I lashed out at some poor nurses,
or is that an induced nightmare
like the seizures I only see
in those vile vagaries
of my mind's own incubus?
A whole day lost,
or two
or three
I've never really known!

Grasping the Edge

Intensive Care Unit:
Monitor sounds, heat, low light,
Icky mask and taped feeding tube.
"No, no, leave that on!"
Endless questions-
Of course I knew the year,
and our Prime Minister.
I wasn't out that long, surely.

I knew it.
I scanned that valley,
Dark and brooding;
The one King David saw.
And felt the fear, the apprehension at least,
As I grasped its rugged edge.
A hand grasped mine and reassured me.
He took my fear
and threw it away.
I spoke with Him, clearer than ever.
"Who'll look after Karen and the kids?"
"I will. You know that."
"OK. If it's my time, Lord, so be it"
Peace.

"But you know I want more time,
want to see my grandkids on my knee,
fulfil something of a destiny
you must have for me.
Though not like Hezekiah;
I will not plead.
If so, so be it!"
He reassures me again,
avows me more time.

Haze of silence over my wife's face,
espied through my half-closed eyes.
She smiles.

TIM HIGGINS

Beauty

Even when you're down on your knees and in the
depths of despair
You can still see beauty
The tear that slides right down your face and hits your
hand with so much grace
then disappears without a trace, that's beauty.
The person lying next to you, you hear their heart it's
beating true.
They've just made perfect love to you, that's beauty
The way a child will look at you, you see the love
shining through and you know that love is just for
you, that's beauty.
The old woman sitting In a chair her face wrinkled
beyond repair, the twinkle in her eye's still there,
That's beauty.
The friend that's standing next to you when you don't
know what to do, no words are spoken, no
need to, that's beauty.

ARLENE FINNEGAN

Washed

Is your clothes clean, where have I been
Does your love flow out, I have been about
Do you pretend to be as white as snow
Is this depression bringing you down low
Have I assurance of your love
Do we fit together like a glove
You were my hour of salvation
Brought to me by your attention
Listen to my story it's changed to a song
You heard my plea after all together along
My vision of angels I found it in you
I'm cinderilla and you my glass shoe

AGNES

Colours

Within my heart there dwells a rainbow
Colours that shimmer and glow
Appearing only when the weeping departs
I become consumed with the rebirth of a gentle
Morning due
This new day is not harsh or cold,
My blue brings a purity that comforts the soul.
There exists a crimson tide, both fury and passion,
It is up to the beholder to decide.
Hidden amongst the blaze of ruby red and streams of
purple and green,
Glimmers, my blissful sunshine, spun with threads of
precious gleaming gold. How can I be sad when the tears
begin to fall, I know that my rainbow and my
Glorious colours will soon come to call.

BARBARA STEELE.

The Day I will never Forget

With tender love I pull the blanket and tuck you in
My heaven sent baby Son, my heart melts with every
Sound you make. I thank God for you.

As I stand now and look at my heaven sent seventeen
Year old Son. His Life Taken.
No blanket just a lid
No teddy bear just my Life, Heart and Soul
I love you with every fibre of my being
As they carry you off,
I plead to God to take me.
But still I stand.
         WHY?

ARLENE FINNEGAN.

Wilted Leaves

Wilted leaves fallen like spent tears,
Salted faces looking hopefully.
Yearn for the slightest smile
A word of comfort, gentle touch.
Nothing given, everything taken
Torn from heart's sinew blind.
Circle circle there is no change.
Mind's glass shattered, worn out woman,
Children bred and flown the nest.
Everyday the same as the one before.
Wilted leaves on the tree of life.
Where is the existence she could have had?
Where is the life she should have had?

LYNDA ROSS.

Wardrobe

The wardrobe is full of your clothes,
How am I going to clear it?
    GOD KNOWS
My mind is full of despair, as I pack
Up your clothes with such care.
The scent of your body so clear,
I know that you're somewhere near,
My eyes they just cannot see but my
Heart says your standing by me, the
Closeness the heartache the pain,
As I put your clothes, in the wardrobe
Again.
This thing, I just cannot do for I could
    NEVER PACK AWAY YOU.

ARLENE FINNEGAN

Writing

Writing
Words on paper
Compelled to mark pages
With raw feelings and emotions
Words sharing my life, a healing process
Sad times, fun times, good times recalled
Living my life in print
My life exposed
Writing

PHILOMENA GALLAGHER

Flash

* * * *The flick of a meteor* * * *
* * * *Splitting the infinite black** * *
* * * * Is over in an instant* * -----**
* * *And cannot be brought back. * *
* * * * But before it entered * * * *
* * * * The domain of the Earth,* ** *
****It travelled a thousand lifetimes* *
* * ** From the place of its birth.*** *

TIM HIGGINS

My Pattern

Eye of the needle then toward the end
Creter on life's journey
Covered by this Ice age
Found only remains of bones in the thaw
Sucked by the vipers and wolves
Buried only by the few

AGNES

Prodigal

You left in anger.
You left that hurtful note.
Saying you loved us,
Yet you loved telling us
so many things.

Your empty room,
I have not entered,
Incompleted of life.

Incomplete
As a father and a man:
I cannot fill the void
In my heart or my house,
Except with anger.
Only anger seems to work,
yet love is always there too,
somehow.

Don't you know
I came back from the dead?
Almost taken from you,
yet you have taken you away.
Don't you know?
Did I come back for this?
You don't believe.
Your brother said he loves you,
and still you don't believe
in miracles?

Are you not Daddy's Girl anymore?
You said yourself
that would never change.

Prodigal Daughter;
You shall wander and spend,
Wonder and spend,
Spend your time and mine,
Until, like the one in that story,
you realise you belong back home.
And stay until the day
We walk the aisle together,
And I hand you over
to another's arm.

"All glorious is the princess
within her chamber.
Her gown is interwoven with gold."

Unbreak my broken sleep.
And like the father in that great story,
I shall continue to watch the horizon.

TIM HIGGINS

Tears For Her Blood

The thirteen year old girl ran up to her bed room, alone she took out the small tub of paracetamols 50 in total. She carefully hung up the high school uniform on the plastic hanger and hesitated, when it came to placing her tie. She placed the uniform inside the wardrobe and touched her primary school tie "ahh better days" she thought, she ripped it off its hanger and placed it on her bed beside the high school tie.

Reaching into her bag, she found the tin of coke, opened it and sat it on the bedside cabinet. Opening the child safety cap of the paracetamols was easy and she tipped the contents in a pile onto the top of her bed. Kneeling at the side of her single bed she prayed asking god to forgive her, to make it quick and painless. Two by two she placed each tablet onto her tongue and swallowed just enough of the drink to wash them down, then took two more and repeated again and again until the tin can was empty, 30 tablets in total had been consumed.

She flexed her fingers, nothing, curled up her toes, nothing. Frustrated she reached for the school ties knotted them together and wrapped it around her left arm, above the elbow, reached into her school bag for her pencil case and found her razor blade. Unwrapping it from the envelope, it glistened, dried blood on one side this she knew was the blunt end, so with the sharp end, the thirteen year old scored along the artery, blood ran slowly but tears ran quickly down her face. Angry, frustrated, desolate, she cried, there was no one to hear her, no one to love her, no one to understand

but this was the last time she would cry for help. She scored and cut, to be certain, 68, 69, 70 yes that would do. Her arm, a mess of cuts, blood and old scars.

Flexing her fingers after unwrapping the ties, nothing, no buzz, no end, nothing. Curling her toes again, nothing.

Desperate she stood on the edge of her bed, tied one end of the tie to the ceiling light flex and the other around her thin young neck, she stepped off the bed, head held up with the tie forcing it back she could see the ties. Slowly the ties came apart one from the other and she fell in a heap onto the floor, head bounced off the mattress.

As she came around from fainting she gathered herself up and slipped into bed crying and sobbing "Why God?", what more had she to do? Soon she was dreaming a vivid vision. She had floated to the ceiling, looked down at herself, her school bag, the ties, the tablets, pencil case everything was as it was in her bedroom. She turned her head away from her sleeping self and found she was floating up a tunnel, a cloud surrounded tunnel towards a light. In a blink of an eye she was walking through the knee high clouds until she came to a small stream, water running over the rocks sparkled like silver over gold. Lifting her eyes to stare beyond the stream she felt the presence of someone coming towards her with a dog, a spaniel was lolloping around the figure.

Then the figure came into clear view and the dog stopped, she realised it was her dog, the dog she had played with fought the cowboys and Indians and cops n robbers. The dog that had followed her and her pram around when they had set up a castle in her childhood home. The dog was

Bouncer, the dog that had to be put down when the girl was eight years old. Her attention focused now on the human figure dressed in a long white night dress and the figure started to wave at her, the girl smiled and waved back. The lady put up her hand palm facing the girl then the hand started to fall and rise "Go back" was the interpretation. "No" the thirteen year old girl thought "No", the hand kept rising and falling.

In the blink of an eye the girl wretched and vomited over her pillow and sheets, she stumbled into the upstairs bathroom and vomited unceasingly into the white porcelain bowl.

In her mind she could only keep saying NO! NO! NO!

AGNES

His Tune

He approached the old tree and
Searched for the right branch.
Tried many pieces until he found the thinnest
Stripped it bare of leaves and bark, whipped
It back and forth like an orchestra
Conductor seeking a perfect F Sharp

Breathing in staccato rhythms between
Clenched teeth, he forced her pleading dance
To his tune, as each piercing
Shrill whistle composed red welts

PHILOMENA GALLAGHER

Useful Contacts for Mental Health & Emotional Well Being

Anxiety / Depression / Phobias / Abuse
ADAPT   (028) 38 347535
            (028) 38 348869

Bereavement
CRUSE   (028) 87 784004
CRUSE Young People's Helpline   0808 808 1677

Men's Support
Men's Advisory Project (MAP)   (028) 90 241929

Mental Health
Action Mental Health   (028) 38 392314
Alzheimers Society   (028) 90 664100
NI Association for Mental Health   (028) 90 328474

Older People
Age Concern Help The Aged NI   (028) 90 245729

Suicide Prevention
Lifeline NI Regional 24/7
Suicide Prevention Helpline   0808 808 8000

S.H.S.C.T. *Project Life Resource Centres*
PIPS Upper Bann   (028) 38 310151
PIPS Newry / Mourne   (028) 30 266195
Southern Area Health Promotion Department   (028) 37 412424

Trauma
Trauma Advisory Panel SHSCT   (028) 30 833074
Victims Support   (028) 90 244039
Wave Trauma Centre   (028) 37 511599

Voluntary / Befriending

Praxis (028) 90 234555
Craigavon / Banbridge
Volunteer Centre (028) 38 342741
S.H.S.C.T. Volunteer Co-Ordinator (028) 38 344973

Emergency

Police, Ambulance, Fire Brigade 999
Southern Area Out of Hours GP 0870 600 600
6 pm – 8 am

Samaritans, Portadown (028) 38 333555
24/7 Helpline 0845 790 9090

Support

S.A.M.M. (Support After Murder and Manslaughter)
Tel: (028) 9442 9009
M: 07890542608